Praise For Gracefully

MW00944049

"The day I met Alicia Coppola was memorable in so many ways...she was beautiful, dramatic, soulful, funny and very real... as our friendship grew I became more aware of the depth of her being... a deep pain and understanding beyond her years... *Gracefully Gone* speaks to her journey… a journey of great love, unbearable pain...a truth and honesty... she makes you laugh, cry and reflect… all the qualities of this amazing woman."

Linda Dano, Emmy Award winning Actress, Talk Show Host, Designer and Author

"I'm a neurologist, and have been in practice for nearly forty years. Recently, I got a call from the daughter of a man who'd been my patient in the early 1980's. She wondered whether I remembered her father...

I couldn't forget her dad; a man who looked like he'd walked off a cinema screen, and was as gracious as he was handsome…Her dad had lived a perfect life until he had a convulsive seizure that lead to the diagnosis of a brain tumor. Initially, he was successfully treated with surgery and radiation therapy.

Once he'd recovered from his tumor treatment, he informed me that he was keeping a journal of his experiences. He wanted to publish his work, but never succeeded. The brain disease wasn't finished with him. His daughter is now finishing his job and fulfilling his wish, more than three decades later. The story intertwines his story with hers, and it says more about the love of child for parent, than it does about tumors or medicine."

Howard B. Reiser, M.D.

"*Gracefully Gone* follows a daughter's journey to try to live life gracefully as she tries to help her father Matt, die gracefully. This is an absolute "must read" for anyone who has tried to find joy in despair or light in darkness."

Kathy Eldon and Amy Eldon Turteltaub
Founders of Creative Visions Foundation
Authors of: *Angel Catcher, Soul Catcher, Love Catcher*, and T*he Journey is The Destination*

"Sometimes a book can change the way we *think* about life, and the way we *live* life as well. This is *Gracefully Gone*: a powerful, engaging, and heartwarming account of a father and daughter's journey to find the power to live and the grace to die. The combination of Alicia and her father's journal exposes a dialogue of similar thoughts, humorous, but often dark stories, and unfinished dreams. A phenomenal read for anyone who has ever lost someone close, questioning his or her own life, and/or seeking guidance for a better way to live."

Jessica Lauren
Founder of The Happiness Movement and 1, 2, 3 Happy
Author of *1,095 Reasons to be Happy: Your Gratitude Journal*

Gone by Mila Jones May 13, 2013

Alicia Coppola
Please follow me on Twitter @alicia_coppola
www.aliciacoppola.wordpress.com

Printed in the United States of America

ISBN 978-1484029114

Gracefully Gone

Alicia Coppola
&
Matthew L. Coppola Sr.

GONE

I see you looking at me
Saying goodbye
Watching the wind blow all the hope away
We try so hard to not cry
But when I think about you my heart breaks
When I left you I was sad
I ran away from home seeking happiness
When I looked back you weren't there to stop me
I like to think that I was mad at you
But it is hard when I love you.

My daughter, Mila Jones
Age 10
May 13, 2013

For my Father
And my daughters
Mila, Esmé and Greta

Author's Note

I mean no harm or disrespect to anyone implied or otherwise in this book. Every word that I have written is a true and accurate account of *my* memory of my early childhood and early adulthood during my father's illness. I cannot speak to the memories of my mother or my brother nor any one else mentioned within this book. These are my memories alone. My father's words are true and accurate to the best of my knowledge. Obviously, he is not here, so we can't ask him. Some names have been altered or not mentioned at all to preserve their privacy.

Contents

Forward

In my wildest literary dreams (where I imagine I am a highly acclaimed author) I would love to imagine that if Simone de Beauvoir was an angry twenty-one year old young woman living in Manhattan in 1992 with a passion for boys, Marlboros and Depeche Mode and she lost her father instead of her mother her memoir *A Very Easy Death* might very well have been titled *Gracefully Gone*.

Gracefully Gone is the fusion of two journals: my father, Matthew L Coppola Sr.'s and mine. My father's journal was written in 1983, three years after his diagnosis with brain cancer.

Mine was written in 1990-1991, roughly eight years later, as he began to die. In *Gracefully Gone* I chronicle my twenty-one year old pursuit of life and all the bitter and amusingly confusing angst that accompanies being twenty-one during the last six months of my father's struggle towards death. In one sense, it is a coming of age tale: from the age of twelve on, I was acutely aware of all things cancer.

I was sent to a New England prep school at fifteen to escape all things cancer only to return after graduating NYU in 1990 to all things cancer. During the six pivotal months between the summer of 1990 and January of 1991, not only did I journal my caretaking of my dad but also our profound love story. At its core, for me, *Gracefully Gone* is very simply a love story: it is my love affair with my dad. I loved, he loved, he died and a bit of me went with him.

When thinking about who might be interested in our story, I was reminded of an article I read in the Los Angeles Times, (November 19, 2003) about Rebecca Brown who wrote *Excerpts From a Family Medical Dictionary*. (University Of Wisconsin Press, 2003) It is a memoir of her mother's death and according to the LA Times "raises an important question; 'How does one make the death of a beloved parent meaningful to strangers?'"

Well, I think I'd like to try and answer that with my own question: how is it not? Everyone I know has either lost or is losing a loved one to cancer. Very few superbly lucky ones have struggled and beaten the cancer monster. The sad fact is in the world we live in today there are no strangers to cancer and there are certainly no strangers to struggle and loss.

What I am hoping, what I am counting on, is that my life, my father's life and our story will be meaningful to strangers; at the very least it will be identifiable, relatable and at times, humorously understandable.

Gracefully Gone is not about death, it is about the journey of a family, specifically the journey of a young girl trying to find her way in the wake of growing up in the looming shadow of cancer. *Gracefully Gone* is to me the literary version of the magical love song "Unforgettable" by Nat King Cole that his daughter Natalie Cole laid her own track to; it is, very simply, a duet.

Perhaps our duet in *Gracefully Gone* is written as a prayer for all the families, all the children too young to understand and for all the victims of this all too often insurmountable war to know they are not alone. Even though my mother and brother went through the same experience as I, we experienced it very differently. It was as if my father was the LOVEBOAT and we three were on our own separate lifeboats surrounding him, each of us handling our grief privately.

Perhaps, if we're really lucky, *Gracefully Gone* might allow someone a little peace and some comfort knowing that even though they are on their own lifeboats they are in an ocean full of them.

"Why were the little girls all frightened
To be just what they are
The boys were told to ask themselves
How high how far
The girls were told to reach the shelves
While the boys were reaching stars
That's why little girls were frightened
To be just what they are."

"Why Do Little Girls"
Harry Chapin

I hid beneath the covers of my bed escaping the ugly maroon bathing suit my mother bought me to wear to my very first boy-girl pool party. It was awful, this bathing suit. I looked at myself in the white wrought-iron full-length mirror my parents had just picked up for me at an antique store. I expected to see a vision; a twelve year old version of the Bain de Soleil model, all sleek and tan and lithe. But no, I looked like someone had drawn a stick figure on a purple paint swatch. My hair was tied back in a sloppy pony, my long arms and legs, which one day *would* be termed sleek and lithe, were simply crazy sticks sticking out from the skinny rectangle that was my torso. This was not right! This was not exactly the image a girl wants to see staring back at her before the biggest pool party of the summer. I couldn't hide fast enough.

I also hid from my father who was waiting, patiently as always, to escort me. It was the summer of 1980. I was twelve. My stomach hurt as it always has, and still does for that matter, when I am anxious about something. In this case, I was nervous about going to *that* party in *that* bathing suit where I would see *that* dreamy boy. As it was, I was already balancing tenuously between popularity and total geekdom. My entire future, whom I sat next to at lunch, and the number of packs of Bubble Yum Bubble Gum, Henry, who was our resident "bad boy," and this twelve-year-old girl's Johnny freaking Depp would give me, hung in this balance. Gum giving was

2

the adolescent equivalent of drink buying and it rested solely on the shoulder straps of that hideous maroon bathing suit. I was fit to be tied. Only one person in this whole unfair world knew how to unravel the macramé that I was. As he entered my room knocking, at least giving the illusion that he respected my preteen privacy, my father was instantly bemused. I had my audience. Upon completion of my woeful tale he looked me over, paused and said, "Well, let's get you something snazzier!"

Instead of a glass slipper, my prince presented me with a black, high cut Capezio swimsuit with a crisscross back! Bubble Yum loomed large in my future. Sadie Hawkins prospects seemed cinched and better yet, I would be the subject of coffee talks for many a bored mother.

My father, Matt, was my first boyfriend. He is the paradigm to which I have tried and most times failed to hold all other men. Tall, athletically slim with dark brown soulful eyes, he was my pinup boy. His lap was meant to comfort and support and his laughter and smile were contagious. With a word or a simple gesture he alone could pacify me. Prone to fits as I was with a propensity for melodrama, he could encourage and mollify me at once. He loved my passion and was amused by my antics. He was my biggest fan.

Four months after this day he was diagnosed with a brain tumor.

The following ten years are a little blurry for me. To this day, fragments of memory flit across my mind like distant relatives who very seldom appear at family gatherings. You know them, but do not recognize them as your own. I have found throughout the writing of this memoir that memories are a lot like fingerprints, uniquely one's own.

I remain in study of my thumb in search of my father.

Chapter One

"And somewhere on your path to glory
You will write the story of a life."

"Story of a Life"
Harry Chapin

①

Dear Alan

When I read Carry Winfield's article in the Sunday
Times Magazine back in April, I was quite impressed
by the number of things that we have in common. I felt
~~besides the facts that~~
I am a M.A.S.H. trivia expert & have seen all of your movies.
that it was then or never that I write for your
assistance. In my mind I wrote it but didn't
                                            my thoughts
quite know if I would ever really put~~s~~ on paper &
send them to you. It wasn't until I returned from my
friend, Harry Chapin's, funeral that I was provoked by his tragic
& untimely death to put into letter form what I had been thinking about
for some time. A Some biography; I am 38 yrs. old & have been
                                   for many years
on the fringe of show business performing in numerous N.Y.
based soap operas & modeling for a great variety of products.
I am also the Vice President of a family owned corporation
dealing in commercial gases & welding products. My wife
                                          her
of 15 years, Linda, is the President of own Home Care
                                three
Corporation, which now operates in 3 states. She
started in our basement & it has now become

5

a multimillion dollar operation. I am very proud of her. She is an example of both your & my belief in equality for women. I have two children, Alicia, now 13 going on 21 who is already in Honor Society & has received A's in her piano & flute state exams, and Matthew 9... who is an excellent student & the center forward on his soccer travel team. Both have done some modeling work with me. Needless to say Linda & I are proud of both of them as I am sure you are of yours.

at 38

X Last October while attending a management seminar in N.Y without prior warning I had two successive grand Mal seizures. I was out for 45 minutes. To make a long story short, it was eventually diagnosed as a brain tumor. The surgery was performed by Dr Rosoloff at N.Y.U Medical Center. He is the subject of the novel "Brain Surgeon." "People fly in from all over the world to have him operate.

③

or them", the admitting clerk told me.

Since my illness I+ has quite a bit of time
to reflect about life & death, & when Harry died so
suddenly, (I saw the smoke from the accident as my office is just
off the L I E, in Westbury) something went off inside me
that I really can't put into words. Maybe you can.

I too came close to death, but I was lucky & with
the help of my wife & family have been able to fight my way
back to my "original" self.   But something is missing
What I have been doing for the last 16 yrs doesn't excite me
anymore & I've been thinking of breaking away.

. There may be a story in my life, something
for you to write, act & direct.   I am a "middle class
adult going about the ordinary business of living" & what
I have been through has "real-life texture & good humor,"
as well as an abundant supply of tears. I been working
! fair? Sharing Reny Jack
on an outline with characterizations.

④

At 38 I we have acheived my "American Dream." just as you have pictured yours.
Linda & I love each other, two happy & loving children
beautiful
a house with a pool, a vacation home in Montauk
overlooking the Ocean, a Porsche etc. - in short all the
material things we all strive for. However, I feel now is the
time for me to move on — Let me explain further!

I have been very curious about my operation in
all of its aspects. For this reason I wrote to Dr. Lensohoff;
requesting to see tapes of my operation. Copy of his reply is
enclosed. One thinks it is only happening to him but
this is not true. Brain tumors, as you know, occur
in people of all ages; they do not descriminate. The
effect that it had on my wife, her parents, my parents,
friends, neighbors, church members even people I didn't even
know was overwhelming. Looking back amidst the
shock & fears & many other emotions expressed, intrigues

8

(5)

me. ~~as a ~~~

I'm hoping it will intrigue you as well.

Sincerely

Walt Coppola

Dear Alan,

When I read Carry Winfield's article in the Sunday Times Magazine back in April, I was quite impressed by the number of things we have in common, besides the fact that I am a *MASH* trivia expert and have seen all your movies. I felt that it was now or never that I write for your assistance. In my mind, I have written this but didn't quite know if I would ever really put my thoughts on paper and send them to you. It wasn't until I returned home from my friend Harry Chapin's funeral that I was provoked by his tragic and untimely death to put into better form what I have been thinking about for some time.

Some biography: I am thirty-eight years old and have been on the fringe of show business for many years. I have performed in numerous New York based Soap Operas and have modeled for a great variety of products and publications. I am also the vice-president of a family owned corporation dealing in commercial gasses and welding products.

My wife of fifteen years, Linda is the president of her own Home Health Care Corporation, which now operates in three states. She started in our basement and it has now become a multi-million dollar operation. I am very proud of her.

She is an example of both your belief and mine, in equality for women. As well as being a smart businesswoman, she's a great mother, a gourmet cook and a foxy lady. She's prettier now than the day I married her.

Our daughter, Alicia has just become a teenager. I believe that should explain everything. She's pretty, talented and an honors student. She never turns off a light and personally supports our local shampoo emporium and the County Water Authority. But she's sure of herself, full of life and that's exactly how we want her to be.

Matthew, our ten-year-old son is the all -American kid. He is the center forward and goalie on his travel soccer team, which is the best in his age group on Long Island. He's a good student, an excellent athlete and a great person. What more could a father ask for?

Last October, while attending a management seminar in Manhattan, without prior warning, I had two successive Grand Mal seizures. To make a long story short, it was eventually diagnosed as a brain tumor. Dr. Joseph Ransohoff performed the surgery at NYU Medical Center. He is the subject of the novel *Brain Surgeon*. People fly in from all over the world to have him "pick their brains." Since my illness, I've had quite a bit of time to reflect about life and death. When Harry died, something went off inside me that I can't really put into words. I came close to death, but I was lucky. With the help of family, I have been able to fight my way back to my "original self."

Something, however, is missing. What I have been doing for the past sixteen years no longer excites me. I'm thinking of breaking away.

I think there is a story in my life, something for you to act in and direct. I have done the "research" and the writing. I am a middle class adult going about the ordinary business of living. What I have been through has "real–life texture and good humor" as well as an abundant supply of tears.

Brain tumors don't discriminate. The effect it has had on my wife, our parents, neighbors, church members and most important, my children has been overwhelming. I am intrigued as a human being by the emotion of this all too common condition. I hope it will intrigue you as well.

Sincerely,

Matt Coppola

Chapter Two

"I know, I gotta go, I gotta go, and I got one last thing and I said it before and I want to say it again. Cancer can take away all my physical abilities. It cannot touch my mind, it cannot touch my heart and it cannot touch my soul. And those three things are going to carry on forever."

Coach Jim Valvano's Speech at The *ESPY Awards*
March 3, 1993

My father's journal entries are dated 1980 -1982 and are italicized. He wrote these entries after he went into remission in 1983.
My journal and memories are dated 1990 - 1991

OCTOBER 27, 1980

I checked into Huntington Hospital for a brain scan and an arteriogram, plus the usual blood and urine analysis. The scan showed nothing unusual. The doctor who performed the test told me he didn't think it was a tumor. We were delighted until Dr. Reiser came into my room. We told him what the doctor said. He asked, "What exactly did he say?" We repeated that the doctor didn't think it was a tumor. He looked skeptically at both of us, doubting that the other doctor had said that. Our elation diminished into fear and frustration because no one really knew.

OCTOBER 28, 1980

The arteriogram came back, the results of which, were nebulous. The doctors agreed that there was a slight edema (swelling) in the suspected area. But that's all they agreed on. Dr. Reiser came into my room to give me his opinion. He said he had good news and bad news. "Give me the bad news first." He thought it could be a low-grade Glioma, probably a one or a two, of unknown pathology and unknown growth rate. That was the bad news. The good news was that if surgery was needed the growth was in a good place. That was the first time I heard the word "surgery." My immediate reaction was that of course I wouldn't require surgery. That was for other people, certainly not for me.

When Linda came we were given two options:

1. Leave it in there and have another CAT Scan done in six months to see if it is indeed growing.

2. Have it surgically removed now before it is too late.

At that point I asked him what he would do if he had this unknown "edema" in <u>his</u> head. He replied that he'd go to Dr. Joe Ransohoff, Chief of Neurosurgery at N.Y.U. Medical Center and let him decide. "He's done wonders with other cases I've referred to him. Hopefully he can do the same for you. If surgery is needed, go to the guy who can do it standing on his ear."

We decided Ransohoff would make the decision. His was to be our final opinion.

OCTOBER 30, 1980

My birthday. We decided to go out to the house in Montauk. It was a trip full of mixed emotions. We were thinking about the outcome of our meeting with Ransohoff. We knew that our "dream house" was so close to becoming a reality. It was all we had ever wanted. But would I be around to enjoy it? We realized that my illness had unalterably changed our attitude toward the future. We met the owner of "our house" for the first time and he showed me how to take care of it. He handed over the key. For the first time we felt the exultation of the "Montauk State of Mind!" It was ours spiritually, if not yet legally. We knew right then that we would go through with the purchase despite our impending circumstance. In a way it was a symbol to us that we had faith in the future. On the way back home I decided to call my neurologist to see if he had made the appointment with Ransohoff on my behalf. "Yes. You're in luck. He'll see you on Monday at one-thirty. However, your first scan wasn't quite right so I have arranged for a second one to be taken tomorrow afternoon." I later found out they had screwed up technically. Not a comfortable feeling.

OCTOBER 31, 1980

I had the second scan. The radiologist said he'd be willing to bet that Ransohoff would say it was nothing. We were temporarily pacified…a moment of peace.

Halloween night: I took in the mailbox so the neighborhood rowdies couldn't destroy it and Linda prepared for the next day, taking care of the money for the Old First Church Annual Fall Fair. I was being practical and Linda, as usual, was taking care of business. Life went on.

NOVEMBER 3, 1980

At 1:30 we sat in Ransohoff's office at the medical center. I was his second appointment of the day as he is in surgery in the morning. Ransohoff's first appointment was there with his wife. He was about 55 and had just undergone his second craniotomy. He had a noticeable limp and his speech was impaired. Linda and I looked at each other in silent communication; "Will this be us?" We spoke with them and they said Ransohoff had taken a tumor from his brain the size of a grapefruit. They praised him and his God given gift. At that point, Ransohoff walked—no—strutted in. He is about 65 years old, trim, about 5 feet tall and weighs about 100 pounds with his hat on. He has closely cropped gray hair (in deference to his patients, whose heads are completely shaved before surgery) and never ever goes anywhere without a cigarette in his mouth or hand, dropping ashes where he pleases. I wondered if he smokes in the operating room! His secretary, Sue, is never far behind. She follows him like a puppy follows its' mother. He is a no-nonsense, matter of fact, blunt but honest man. He is the only 5-foot giant I have ever met.

When we entered his inner office with my portfolio of X-rays, he was on the phone. With a cigarette in his free hand, he motioned us to sit. He asked to see my X-rays. I told him I was the only working model with a portfolio of the inside as well as the outside. He didn't laugh.

16

He stuck the pictures against the backlight, asked me what happened and listened intently as I told him about the seizure. He said he was fairly sure what had caused it but wanted to confirm it with his radiologist. He immediately called Dr. Ling, Chief of Radiology, and told him he was going to send me down to see him.

We walked down a long corridor to the radiation department and saw dozens of people waiting. We were surprised when a nurse quickly referred me to another nurse who was waiting for my X-rays. She offered us coffee and said "He really wants to take his time and study these in order to make the correct diagnosis." I felt very comforted by that. Here was the Chief of Radiology in a teaching hospital willing to devote the necessary time to evaluate my X-rays simply because Ransohoff had asked him to. I paced back and forth for almost a half an hour while Linda sat there with her legs crossed, top leg going up and down a mile a minute. Dr. Ling finally came out and asked, "How did this manifest itself?" I wasn't sure what he meant, so I said, "What do you mean?"

"What caused you to seek help?"

"I had a seizure."

"I see," he said.

"What do you think?" I asked.

"I already told him what I think," as he pointed upward. "He should be the one to tell you."

Linda's knees got weak and mine weren't any stronger, but I had to hold her up. Dr. Ling returned my portfolio and sent us back up to Ransohoff.

By this time his office was packed, but as soon as he saw us through his partially opened door he waved us into his inner office with his cigarette, again while he was on the phone. He got off the phone, and keeping the others waiting, he immediately came in to see us. "Life is shit!" He said. Linda, who never smokes, asked him for a cigarette and couldn't light it because her hands were shaking so badly.

"It's a tumor, low grade, don't know how fast it's growing. It's been there for about ten years and now it's caused a seizure. 17

Something should be done about it. It's in a good spot. I can get in and get it out and you'll be back to work in a couple of months."

"Will I still be able to play basketball?" I asked, fearfully remembering the man I met earlier in his office.

"Sure. You a jock? I like jocks."

I asked him how soon he could do it. "As soon as a bed is available at the hospital. Think about it. You're a young man, you'll recover quickly."

"Could you do it in Huntington Hospital?"

"No, I work with my own team in my own shop. You think about it. And let me know what you decide."

The ride down the elevator was silent. We got our car and drove still in silence until we paid the toll at the midtown Tunnel.

"Matt, this is your decision, this is one that is yours and only yours. Whatever it is, I will go along with it 100%." We both started crying because _finally_ someone had said, "This is what it is, I can help you. You will be fine." We told our families. They reacted the way you would expect loving families to react when hearing that a member of their family has a brain tumor.

NOVEMBER 5, 1980

We met with our attorney who was to handle the purchase of the Montauk house. A lifelong friend, he was aware of our situation. He gave us a great deal of moral support when we needed it most as well as love and understanding. He made the day normal for us. For a few hours we were ourselves again.

By the end of the day the house was ours. We took the children out to dinner to celebrate. Were we celebrating the purchase of the house or the refusal to give up hope for our lives?

NOVEMBER 11, 1980

A holiday. Veterans Day. We were anxious to get out to our "New Home." We wanted to be alone so we left the kids with my mother and drove out. It was just as we thought it would be, quiet,

18

serene, simple and <u>ours</u>. I remember going over each item the former owner had told me about, making sure I understood. It was so important to me.

That night the moon hung over the horizon shimmering its light onto the water and reflecting it to our deck. The view was even more magnificent than we had expected. As usual, we chose Montauk as the place to make all our crucial decisions. From a phone booth in the Montauk circle, I told Dr. Ransohoff to get me a room. It was a cold, damp and dreary day. I'll never forget it. After the call we went back to the house and made love. For the first time in my life I was impotent. I knew it was the culmination of the past few weeks of stress and emotional upset concerning my decision about surgery. I also knew at that time that I had made the right decision. I felt I'd rather have the tumor removed and take my chances than face a life knowing I might not be able to please my wife or myself.

NOVEMBER 13, 1980

I was in the city for a modeling job. When I called the office there was a message for me to call Ransohoff. I was scheduled to be at the hospital the following day at 12:30 PM. I told Linda. "Oh my God, so soon?" I was more optimistic about it. I had complete faith in my surgeon and was relieved that I didn't have to wait any longer.

When I got home I told the children that I had to go to the hospital for a while and that I wanted them to take care of their mother while I was gone. Alicia reacted with acceptance. Matthew said nothing. We were not to see him smile for a long time.

NOVEMBER 15, 1980

My new modeling composites were finished and I wanted to give them to my agent before I entered the hospital. I told him to book me out for a couple of months. I guess planning for the future made me feel there would be one.

19

When I finally arrived at the hospital I told the nurse who admitted me that Ransohoff was my surgeon. "People fly in from all over the world to get his opinion." If I had any lingering doubts about him, her words eliminated them.

All of Ransohoff's patients are on the east wing of the 11th floor, the neurosurgery floor. His Chief Resident is Dr. Nancy Epstein. She was to be Ransohoff's assistant during surgery. She too, was no nonsense, patterned after Ransohoff in manner, but his opposite in appearance: she was tall, thin with long dark hair. She was all business as she made the rounds, barking out orders for the interns. She knew her job well and was damned good at it. She made no effort to become my friend, even though I tried to become hers. I guess detachment is a necessity; a large percentage of patients never fully recover and most of them die.

My surgery wasn't scheduled until the following Tuesday, November 18. There were tests scheduled for Monday to pinpoint the exact location of the tumor for the surgeons. The staff continued my Dilantin to prevent any further seizures, added Phenobarbital, a depressant to calm me down, steroids to reduce the swelling after surgery and a milky white substance to prevent all of these drugs from giving me a hole in my stomach. Other than that, I had Friday and the weekend to sit around and think about my surgery. Friday night during rounds, Ransohoff came in. "You're free for the weekend. Go out and have a good time. Just leave any time after morning medication and be back for night medication." Free for the weekend? Have a good time?

Saturday while I was waiting for Linda to come in, a nurse asked if I minded if my new roommate smoked. "Yes, I mind." "Okay, when you come back tonight you'll be in the next room down the hall." I thought it was strange that someone would be allowed to smoke in the hospital.

Linda came in after lunch (contrary to popular opinion I liked hospital food!) and we went to Bloomingdales, Lord &Taylor and Saks. We didn't buy anything, but it was good to get out of the hospital and occupy our minds with something other than the impending surgery. We had a marvelous day together but I could tell she was going through hell. Actually, it was worse for her than it was for me. She had a business to run, children to take care of, me to visit 47 miles away and a household to run all by herself. She later told me that she swore the Porsche knew its own way home and back to the hospital because half the time she was in a stupor. I focused my concerns on her. I was sure I'd be okay, I was less sure about her.

We returned to find two new patients in my old room. We were also met with pandemonium. One patient was an anesthesiologist at a hospital in Amityville and the other, the smoker, was in a violent seizure. The anesthesiologist tried to help him, to no avail. The nurse rushed in followed by the emergency team who arrived just about the same time we did. We sat in the foyer with this man's parents and wife while they worked on him. We learned that he had been through a series of operations that had left him paralyzed from the neck down and was now back for another. He was just 29 years old and had a small baby. We talked for about ten minutes and could hear the team working furiously on him. Finally, a young nurse, visibly shaken, came over to his wife with tears in her eyes, "He didn't make it."

It was one of the saddest scenes we had ever seen. Neither one of us will ever forget it. I found out later why the doctor permitted him to smoke. He had no time left. The anesthesiologist later told me that during his short stay with him, the smoker told him that he couldn't go on living a life in and out of hospitals. He was no good to his wife, wasn't a father to his child and wished he were dead. I guess the Lord gave him his wish and put him out of his misery. We all felt so sorry for his wife and family, but I think they were relieved in their sadness. Finally it was all over. I was embarrassingly relieved that I had switched rooms. All this time I could see the pressure building up in Linda and this incident certainly didn't help. She couldn't admit it at the time, but she was really scared.

Sunday morning came and went as I waited for Linda to arrive. I realized she had a lot of juggling to do with the children, they couldn't stay alone and thank God both sets of parents and

Karen, her secretary, volunteered to stay with them. She was also involved with the Church Choir and was obligated to sing the 11:00 AM service every Sunday. I think she used that time in church to gain spiritual strength to carry her through this ordeal.

NOVEMBER 17, 1980

My best friend, Jon, had made arrangements for us to have an early dinner at the Tavern on the Green in Central Park. His wife Lynn had the flu and didn't want to infect me before surgery. So it would just be the three of us. From my window, I could see the main entrance on First Avenue. I watched for both of them. I recall so many times during my stay looking out of the hospital at the 59th Street and George Washington Bridges all lit up and wondering what a view like that would have cost me on the "outside." I knew it couldn't cost me as much as it was on the "inside."

Linda finally arrived, her face mirroring her pain and anxiety and smelling like Shalimar, her signature fragrance. It usually aroused me. This time I felt nothing. We are both survivors. We would pull through this thing one way or another. She agreed, but it was still shaky.

Jon arrived with a small clock radio for me to pass the time of day. He always had some unique doodad or gadget for me – this was one of them. Jon and I have been friends ever since our wives, who were college roommates, brought us together fifteen years ago. Linda and I have known each other since the eighth grade. We went all the way through high school together without ever dating. One August afternoon after we had both finished college; I was riding my scooter and happened to pass her house. I saw her parents on the lawn and stopped to chat with them and inquired about Linda. "She's just returned from her College Choirs' tour of Europe and is bored stiff. Why don't you go up there and cheer her up." (Wise woman, my mother-in-law.) I asked her out that night. She said she knew that night I would be her husband. It took me almost two years to be convinced!

22   We then proceeded to the Tavern on the Green, a favorite

place, especially during the holiday season with all the Christmas decorations. We sat in the crystal room and made light of the impending surgery. It was polite banter and levity, and we had a good time but the undercurrent was nervous trepidation. We toasted to the skill of my surgeons. When we finished dinner Jon dropped us back at the hospital and I said goodnight to Linda in the lobby. I told her to go home and get a good night's sleep. We embraced each other silently as tears rolled down our cheeks. Then she said something I'll never forget: "Could you put me in your pocket Schmoo?" "I'd love to," I replied, "but I don't think I'm gonna have a pocket."

After she left I was alone and I was somehow relieved. It was up to me now to get mentally prepared for my surgery. An hour passed. An intern came in to put a catheter in my arm. He fished it through to my heart so that they could monitor my vital signs during surgery. I spoke with him while he was doing it. I was curious, nothing more. He then inserted a urinary catheter. I had heard that I would experience excruciating pain, but I wasn't bothered by it at all. After he left, the social worker came in to tell me how depressing my stay would be and to give her a call if I needed anything. I had been there five days and did not need to be reminded how depressing it was. But it was about time she came around!

After she left an orderly came in to shave my head. I remember thinking at the time; "There goes my modeling career!" When he finally left, I couldn't control my curiosity to see my baldhead. So I grabbed my I.V. pole, monitoring and urinary catheters and wobbled over to the bathroom mirror to see what I looked like. I thought I looked pretty good as a baldy!

I no sooner got back to bed, than my anesthesiologist came in and said laughingly "All right, which one of you good looking guys is the victim?" I said I was as if he didn't know. He explained what the procedure would be the next morning, gave me a sedative and before I had a chance to say a prayer, I was asleep.

They woke me up at 5:45 AM to take me down to surgery.

At 6:30 they transferred me to a gurney and wheeled me out to the elevator and I was on my way. No turning back now. I said the Act of Contrition and thought to myself, "Let's go for it."

Surgery was on the 6th floor. I remember waiting in line in the surgery hallway. We were stacked up like airplanes waiting on the runway to take off. I recall the big clock in the hallway reading 7:45 before they wheeled me into a white, white, cold, cold room. The green gowns the doctors and nurses wore contrasted so starkly with the whiteness of the room. There was a lot of activity going on as they prepared for surgery. They slid me onto the operating table. The anesthesiologist put a catheter in my leg. I asked him what that was for and he said it was Sodium Pentothal. At that point I didn't know whether they were going to question me or operate on me! Dr. Epstein appeared and told me Ransohoff was outside prepping and that the anesthesiologist was going to put me under. He appeared form behind my head and said,

"How are you doing, Matthew?"

"Fine so far, Doc."

"Good, I'm going to put this mask over your nose now and I want you to inhale, okay?"

"Ok…" Out.

I'm told the surgery took just over five hours. Ransohoff told Linda to be there around 10:30 am. She came with her parents and Lynn and Jon. Linda told my parents to stay home, as she didn't think my mom could handle it. She had just gone through some heart problems of her own. Linda had faith that everything would be all right, but by the time Ransohoff sauntered out at around 12:45, her nerves were shot. He seemed all refreshed, cleanly shaven and apparently had made some calls. I don't think he realized they had been there since 10:30.

They surrounded him in anticipation. Had I survived the operation? Seeing concern in Linda's face he said,

"He's all right. Don't worry. He'll be alright."

"Will he be alright?"

"Yes, it was just as I expected. I removed it. I removed the tumor…He will need radiation, however. I didn't want to go too deep and impede his speech. So the radiation will get what I didn't."

"Thank God. But, will he be alright?"

"Yes, I think by the color that it was benign, but I cannot be sure. We'll have the results in a few days."

"But you're sure he'll be alright, doctor?"

"Yes but there are no guarantees in life. I got the tumor out. The rest is up to him. Don't read into what I've said."

"I realize that." And she walked to the window sobbing.

Jon interrupted, "Lin, he said he was going to be fine."

Her father said," He's going to be fine, didn't you just hear him say that? What's the matter? He just told you he will be fine." She just sat there and cried.

After surgery, I was taken to the ICU on 11E and placed on oxygen. By that evening I was off oxygen and Linda came to see me and recalls I had a funny grin on my face, like I was still out of it. Dr. Epstein came by. "How're you doing, Matt? Still have trouble getting the words out? How're you doing, can you talk yet?" Linda stepped outside the door with her and asked, "Why do you keep asking him why he can't get the words out?" Epstein said, "It's normal to ask since we went in very close to the speech area." She walked away, leaving Linda with the fear she would never be able to hear my voice again.

Suddenly the doors to the ICU swung open by a nurse frantically calling for Epstein. Linda didn't know what was going on until she peeked into the ICU and saw them working on me as I heaved up and down on the bed. I was having another seizure. She ran over to her father, trembling and terrified, with visions of last Saturday nights' smoker in her head, wondering if this was the end.

Her father walked her over to the waiting area and sat her down. Ransohoff came over to them and said to her father," Take her home." He then ordered a nurse to give her a Valium.

"He'll be alright. This sometimes happens after surgery."

"You weren't here Saturday night when your smoker

died." Linda cried back.

"All right. All right." He disappeared back into ICU.

Jon went to get Linda some water. When he returned she was shaking so violently he had to hold her hands steady to get her to drink. She took the Valium and finally calmed down.

She doesn't remember the ride home with her parents, but she does remember asking them to come in with her to face the children. Luckily, they were asleep.

Linda took a long soothing shower, went into the den and made herself a stiff drink. She sat in quiet desperation until she finally fell asleep on the couch.

NOVEMBER 20, 1980

I stayed in the ICU until Thursday morning. The doctors decided I was doing so well that I didn't need ICU anymore. Instead they recommended private nursing around the clock.

It soon became obvious why I needed this care. While physically I was doing fine, mentally I was not equipped to be on my own. I was frightened, had heart palpitations and needed the psychological support these nurses could provide.

NOVEMBER 21, 1980

By Friday afternoon the nurses had been dismissed, I was up and around and able to go to the toilet unassisted. I was still hooked up to the IV pole however. I hadn't shaved since I entered the hospital a week before and by this time looked like a grub. So I asked Jon, who visited every day, to bring me some shaving cream and a razor. He had been bugging me to shave and I had resisted. There's something about being bald that makes you want to grow a beard or a mustache. It may be psychological, but have you ever noticed how many bald or balding men have beards? Anyway, he arrived at around noon with the shaving gear and a hot corned beef on rye from Max's Stars Deli on Third Ave. I ate the sandwich after I had my regular hospital lunch. I had a voracious appetite.

One thing I don't understand – I lost 12 pounds during my stay, while eating everything in sight – the tumor must have been very dense!

Jon made this big production about me shaving. He got me hot towels to heat and soften my beard and the whole bit. I disappeared into the bathroom looking really grubby. When I applied the shaving cream I lost my nerve. I decided I'd keep the beard until I could model again. All I did was trim it neatly around the sides, upper lip and under the chin near the neck.

I emerged from the bathroom with a towel covering my face, like a bandit in the old Westerns as I approached Jon. After I got settled back in bed I removed the towel. He laughed and said, "You look exactly like you did before you shaved! You look exactly the same! What did you make me buy all that stuff for?" I shrugged my shoulders and said, "I don't know," with a big smile on my bearded face.

NOVEMBER 24, 1980

One of the "status symbols" in the hospital for craniotomy patients was getting sanitary skullcap after the stitches were removed. This was a piece of sanitary hose, which rolled off a spool. It was cut to size and was closed at the top by a rubber band. It served two purposes. The first was obvious, to protect the incision against infection. The second was not so obvious, to keep the head warm. You'd be surprised how much body heat you lose through the top of your head, especially after you've been shaved.

The left side of my head was very swollen with fluid. I had been stitched from below the center of my forehead straight up to the top center of my head where it made a right turn and went straight down to just in front of my left ear. They left the stitches in for about a week, checking them daily to make sure there was no infection. When they started to take them out, I was awarded my sterile stocking cap. The only place I had a scab was in the middle of my forehead, but I was afraid to pick it off. When I returned to the hospital a week after I was discharged, Ransohoff said something to the effect that they should have removed it while I was still in the hospital. He did it right then and there. As it turns out, that's the only place that shows a jagged scar. I think it gives me a "macho" look.

Even though I was still hooked up to the IV pole, I was free to roam the floor. I would wake at 5:30 AM and walk from 11E to 11W, which was about 100 yards from end to end. It was still dark out and the halls were eerie. I did this every morning and afternoon trying to build up my strength. The nurses commented that I was really doing well. Very few patients exhibited the determination that I had.

I had this deep pain, a cramp in my right calf bothering me and I was trying to walk it out. The more I walked the more it hurt. I was determined to conquer it. Every morning with unwavering perseverance, I would walk the outer perimeter of the hallways for at least a half an hour. I was determined to get back into shape as soon as possible. At one point I thought I had phlebitis and asked to have it checked out. The doctor came with a Thromboscope, which amplifies the sound of blood as it rushes through the veins. He said I definitely did not have phlebitis and it was good for me to continue to walk. I didn't believe him. I told Jon about it. He promptly went to the nursing station and asked to see my chart. Surprisingly, they let him see it. The chart showed no phlebitis and he convinced me. I returned to walking. It probably had to do with the steroids they were giving me.

At another point during my stay I hallucinated that Ransohoff returned to my room after rounds and told me that he didn't get the entire tumor out. That it might spread. I told Linda about it. She disagreed with me. When Ransohoff came in that night, she asked him in front of Jon, her parents and me if what I was saying could be true. "Me? Come back after rounds, you've got to be kidding. I have the tumor downstairs in a jar. You want to see it? I got it all. It was a slight mixture. Anything else in there will have to be taken care of by radiation." That was the first time I realized I would have to undergo radiation treatment. Up until then I thought I'd have the operation, take the medication for a year or two and be done with it. It doesn't work that way. You either get radiation, chemotherapy or both. In my case radiation was all that I needed. Linda knew this all along but didn't reveal it.

I had made such a point of not wanting radiation due to what I thought would be permanent hair loss that Linda was afraid to tell me. Now that Ransohoff told me – I had to accept it. My fears were false. Most of my hair has grown back.

NOVEMBER 27, 1980

Thanksgiving Day. It was now nine days after surgery. The intern came in to remove the last of my stitches. It was the first time we let the children come to see me since I entered the hospital. I got all dressed up in my "good PJ's" and waited for them at the elevator. When they appeared, all the pent up emotion vented in a burst of tears, happiness and relief. It was truly an exhilarating and cathartic reunion. We went back to the room and settled down to questions about schoolwork, boys that Alicia was "dating" (a new one every day) and soccer. Matt said that he was playing okay, but that he missed me and wanted me to come home. I told him I'd be home Sunday and that cheered him up.

They were curious about my scar and naturally wanted to touch it. I let them, warning them of course, that it was still very tender and full of fluid. We sat there all afternoon, talking, playing games and watching TV. Matt brought in a whole bag of handmade get well cards from his class. I put every one of them up on the wall for all to see.

My brother-in-law had invited them over for Thanksgiving dinner, so they left at about five. But not before I took them around the floor, introducing them to the nurses who cared for my fellow inmates and me and not before Ransohoff came in to wish his patients a happy Thanksgiving. He could have taken the day off. After all, it was a holiday. He didn't. That's dedication.

NOVEMBER 30, 1980

Ransohoff said he'd spring me just before noon on
Sunday. I was packed and ready to go right after breakfast. I still
had a couple of hours to kill before Linda arrived. I removed all
the cards from the wall, which by this time had no space left and
neatly packed them in a plastic bag along with other letters and
small gifts. (I still have the cards and letters and will keep them as
a reminder of how many people cared for me in my time of need.) I
still had candy and flowers and fruit left. I made my rounds saying
goodbye to the staff and other patients. I gave them each a gift in
honor of my appreciation for caring for me – or a remembrance of
a shared experience. However dubious it may have been.
Linda finally arrived. I saw her pull in with her
"Schmoomobile" from my room, 11 stories up. By this time I was
incredibly anxious to leave and never look back. I greeted her
at the elevator. My bags were outside my room. We went to the
nursing station to get released, expecting someone official like
a doctor, to sign us out. Instead a male nurse who was on duty
handed me my medication and explained that I should take it
in the morning and evening before I go to bed. It seemed to me
that the dosage was less than I had been getting while I was in
the hospital. I questioned it at the time. He said, "That's what the
doctor ordered." I figured they got the tumor out and I didn't need
as much medication. We picked up my things and calmly walked
over to the elevator and pressed the button to freedom.
I remember my first breath of fresh air as we emerged from
the hospital. It was good to be out. It was good to be alive. As we
drove home Linda told me the kids were at soccer tryouts. "Let's
stop there and see them before we go home." I said. "Are you sure?"
She asked. "Yes." We arrived as they were scrimmaging. As we
approached, Matt immediately ran over to us and gave me a big
hug. He was smiling for the first time in a month. Alicia was not far
behind. One by one the team parents came over to us to ask how I
was feeling. Again the emotions ran away with us. There we were
on a soccer field on a brisk November day – thirty nine-year-

30

olds and their parents – all with tears in our eyes because we all realized it could have been any one of us. But it had been me and I was with my wife and children, alive.

Chapter Three

"The intense people have never fit into any society.
It's not just now. But, they are the artists, the creators,
The life enhancers always."

May Sarton[1]

Father, father, burning bright
    In the darkness of the night-
    Blake's not here, no only me
    Searching for your divinity.
Daddy, daddy still in my sight
    Spiraling into the light.
    Did you feel it?
    Did you know?
    This was to be your final bow?
What was the first thing
    You thought of
    When the doctor sentenced you?
    Was it your life as a boy
     In Brooklyn
    An altar boy on Avenue U;
Was it your dream to be a doctor?
    How ironic if that were true.
    Banging gavels on prescription pads-
    Death verdicts passed by you.
Or was it an actor on the TV screen?
    Soap operas I think it was.
    Pre-canon bluebooks told the truth
    Because the church says it does.

Could it be your money house?
        The girl you called your Schmoo.
        Or might it be the children,
        We so young, who cared for you?
Did you know aphasic mouths contort?
        To scream in pain
        To whisper love
        To beg for life's support.
And, as you lay there dying-
        Lying lonely on your bed,
        With nothing but your tumor
        Growing silently in your head...
Did your brain talk to your tumor?
        While it swallowed you,
        Did you tell it about the fear?
        That Jesus would save you...
And,
        Did you taste the pills?
        The radiation in high doses
        Did you hate the smile
        The one the doctor forces?
And,
        Did you see wife weeping?
        See the children sneaking in,
        To see this wax gray monster
        Trying desperately to win.

                    Alicia Coppola -1986

I was emotionally orphaned at twelve. Even before cancer literally took my father's life, it took my otherwise idyllic and peaceful childhood. It left my brother Matthew and me in the often times negligent foster care of my mother who, along with her glasses of wine, wandered the halls like she was doing time. She was imprisoned by her grief. Cut off from us to wallow and reel at what had become of her love, her life. We were left to watch, to hold her hand, clutching for each other all the while wondering who was going to hold ours.

The day of my father's first grand mal seizure, I had come off the school bus at my stop and saw my grandfather waiting for me in his car.

"Something has happened to your father. Go inside the house, go downstairs and get your mother. Don't tell her what it is. Just tell her I am waiting for her upstairs."

My mother ran a large, irony of ironies, healthcare company out of our basement. In order to get to my mother, I had to negotiate all the desks that sat her secretaries and ask them to get her.

"Tell him to wait a minute. I'm on a call." My mother briskly stated.

Up the stairs I went to deliver this news to my grandfather who quickly descended the stairs himself to get her. I followed and from my vantage, I viewed my mother silently fall apart. It is a look I will never forget, as it is one I have come to know very well: her whole face slackens, tears gather but never fall, hands shakily light the first or fifth cigarette of many that shroud her in a cloak of smoke that she stupidly thinks cover her like a curtain. She travels deep inside herself where she feels safe and closes off to everything around her, which at the time included me.

One of my mother's secretaries Karen stayed with us that afternoon. A few hours after she left, my brother and I found my mother lying in the den, an empty bottle of Scotch by her side. We dragged her off the couch and into her bedroom. Our meal that night was the first of many grilled cheese sandwiches my eight-year-old brother would make for us for dinner.

A few nights later, my father told us his awful secret at the kitchen table where all things important and trivial were discussed. I wasn't twelve anymore. I left the kitchen table and in the time in took me to get to our family's library I was ageless. I sat on the couch, looking at the books, searching through my book bag to get that night's homework that I no longer saw the point to doing. I was too old for homework. I was too old to go to school. I was suddenly older than the musty books that lived on the shelves. I knew everything they had to tell me, I knew nothing. I knew I would never again know what 12 felt like, or what being a child felt like for that matter. I was ageless. I was ageless and old. I had the face and body of a preteen girl and the heavy spirit of an eighty-year-old woman.

It was fitting and providential that I should choose to go into the library that night, as that room and all it held became my solace and my escape. I was always a reader, but now I became positively enmeshed in books. With each new title yet another and another world engulfed me and I no longer had to live in mine. It was all I had. Although my house was full of people, they were not there for me. They worked for my mother. Although I spent much of my days at school surrounded by even more people, they were not there for me.

And, although I would come home to my parents, they were not there for me. I was surrounded by people and yet no one, it seemed, saw me.

My brother was lucky. As boys are wont to do, they can start lifelong friendships over a soccer ball and my brother was no exception. He had friends from preschool and these boys these families took him in, if not literally, than figuratively. He had many moms feeding him, consoling him if he opened up enough to let them and many homes to call his own. I was not so fortunate. Little girls don't see another little girl in pain, hurting, crying, longing for a father that was not yet dead but on his way. They don't see a human being in need of a friend, a shoulder, a warm embrace, and a kind word. Little girls see prey. Emotional weakness in a twelve-year-old girl is akin to a gazelle with a twisted ankle lying just outside a lion's den. I wish I could say I had one best friend who saved me, who provided a haven of comfort from everything else. But I can't. I had friends. I had one in particular but as I have come to understand, a childhood best girlfriend is nothing more than an enemy keeping her close.

I tried to fit in, to be seen. I tried hard to talk about boys and makeup and the one girl who was now a slut because my so-called "best friend" said so. I even pretended, to my shame, that I hated that girl, who I really didn't even know, so I would be accepted into this evil coven; so I could belong to something. Anything. These little things, the makeup, boys, clothes and the sluts, became everything. Everything I had to hold on to. But the more I tried to fit, the faster my hold, the less I fit in. It was almost as if these girls knew I was using their ridiculousness, their nastiness to hide and, slowly, I became the one they talked about. I became the girl they snubbed in the halls. I was on the receiving end of the silent aggression middle-class, white girls use to terrorize instead of fists. I took the elbows and nasty sneers in the halls. I sat alone at lunch amid the whispers and glances and laughter in my direction. They knew my Achilles' heel and ran with it…I was the one whose father was dying and wasn't it a shame hee hee hee...

I went to the "best friend's" house and from there to a family reunion party they were going to. I had to go. My mother was with my father in the hospital and my brother went to one of his "vacation homes" as I liked to call them. No one else could watch me. My grandparents were away and I was too old to need a baby sitter and too young to stay by myself. So I went and watched my friend with her family and sat at their table and ate their food, watched them dance with each other, laughing, laughing and became strangely possessed by a great need for them to adopt me. The deejay played "Daddy's Little Girl" and I thought I would go out of my head when the "best friend's" dad asked her to dance. I got up and went to the hallway where I saw a pay phone from one of my earlier bathroom trips and picked up the receiver. I wanted to call my father, but I didn't know if I had one anymore and I didn't want to know. I held onto the phone and thought that maybe if I wanted it enough, my father's voice would just be there when I put the receiver to my ear. Or that maybe, if I really wanted it bad enough, he would walk through the door, swoop me into his arms and dance with me to this song while my friend looked on hoping we would adopt her.

Nothing happened. I walked away from the phone and saw my friend, dancing with her father, taking an exceptionally, yet subtle thrill at my pain. I think the only person who remotely understood me that night was her father: For that one moment since my father's illness, I had a glimmer of what it felt like to be grateful for someone's empathy.

I remember going to school the next day and seeing the "best friend" in the hallways, holding court over the throng of her admirers. I think deep down she felt for what I had seen and felt the night before, but the only thing she displayed was the conceit of familial wholeness that she blatantly lauded over me.

Bitch.

I think I wafted through the schools halls that day: ghost-like, drifting from class to class awaiting the end of school bell like a death row inmate awaits the governor's reprieve. Once home, I locked myself into my bedroom, sat right by my door, listening to my family in the other room watching TV, while I held a knife I had stolen from the kitchen wondering what it would feel like if I just simply stabbed myself. Just stuck it right in my gut. Right where it hurts all the time. Would there be blood? Would the pain be worse than it already was? Would my family take a break from their TV show and wondering where I was, come and discover me dead on my bedroom floor with a knife sticking out of my stomach? Would they care?

Perhaps it would be a relief that they wouldn't have to deal with my father's disease and an emotionally crippled and obviously psychologically disturbed daughter at the same time. I might be doing everyone a great big favor. Mostly, I thought, because even then I knew this to be true, I would be doing myself a favor. Ending my own life so I wouldn't have to see the end of my father's. The cold blade was nice. It was cool and comforting. In its shiny metal, it reflected back exactly what I was, distorted. I welcomed the pain it would inflict. I welcomed any pain that didn't come from within.

I didn't cut myself that day or any day since. My fascination with knives was conceived and aborted in that moment and I simply got up from my floor, walked the knife into the kitchen, put it back in its drawer and told my parents I couldn't go back to that school. Can't say they were shocked. Can't say they didn't see this coming. I think they knew what my father's illness was doing to us, to me and didn't know how to help me. My brother had his friends and his sports. I had a kitchen knife.

My mother wrung her hands, hovering over me as I lay on our living room couch crying that I simply couldn't go back. I didn't really have friends and the ones I did have were useless and mean.

"What are we going to do, Matt?" My mother asked my father. "What are we going to do with her? This school thing has been going on too long. It has to stop."

It wasn't her fault that she thought my breakdowns were all about school. I think I placed the entire onus on that because I didn't know how to say I am scared daddy's dying and I don't want to be left. I don't want him to leave me. I am afraid of what I am going to see when he dies and mostly I am afraid of feeling like I am feeling right now forever.

My father's suggestion was that we look into other schools. This began our search into private schools, boarding schools in particular. I don't know if he knew my real fears, but I think he did. I think my father was looking out for me. I think my father was the only one who ever really understood me. He was after all, the Italian in the family and possessed all the passion that came with his background. I inherited that passion from him. My mother possessed the German stoicism. What my mother hid, he felt openly.

My father was the father every kid, even those that had a father of their own would go to for just about everything. If a kid wanted to know how to swim, he came to my father. Dive? Mow lawn? Play soccer, baseball, and basketball? Came to my father. When the leaves began dropping in mid-October, our friends would come over to help rake because they knew my father would take us all to Friendly's our local ice cream parlor/diner, for ice cream sundaes. My father was the Piped Piper of the children of Huntington.

My Uncle Jon tells the story of one night during the summer of 1980, right before my father's diagnosis. My parents and Aunt Lynn (my mother's best college friend) and her husband Jon, were having dinner and were in the middle of a very serious, adult conversation. The doorbell rang and my father got up from the table, mid sentence to answer the door. There were about eight, waist high kids on our stoop asking if Mr. Coppola could come out to play! Uncle Jon says my Dad turned around, looked at my mother and said, "We done here?

Can I go out because I wanna play?" Jon says my father stayed outside shooting hoops and playing with these children until their own mothers called them home. This was not unusual. Not only did the kids come to my father for fun, but they also came when in trouble. I think they knew my father wouldn't judge, but would listen and offer any help he could.

One weekend day, my brother and his friends were playing at the local elementary school, which was two blocks around the corner from our house. They were playing baseball. When my brother Matthew ran and jumped to catch a fly ball, he landed on a piece of wire sticking up from the school's chain link fence. The wire went thru his skin and he was literally hanging by his right arm from the fence. All the other little boys had the presence of mind to hold Matthew up from his butt, to keep his weight off his arm. They yelled to another boy to run and get help. The kid could have run to the first house he saw, but he didn't. He ran all the way to our house to get my father, because he knew my father would come running immediately and take care of everything. Suffice to say when my father became ill, many children suffered.

As far as I was concerned, my father knew my going away to boarding school was not the best solution. I would be away from him when we didn't know what kind of time line we were dealing with. He would miss me. He would miss my growing up and the things that happen to teenage girls when we grow up. Much of what he was going to miss, I am sure he looked forward to missing! But I think somewhere inside him he knew it was best for me to not be anymore of a witness to his demise than I already was. As it was, unbeknownst to my mother, my father was already allowing me to drive way before I was legal so that in the event he had a mini vocal or grand mal seizure while driving, I could take over. I think he knew that just that alone might be too much responsibility for me to bear.

As if I didn't have enough trouble at school already and because I had confided, stupidly in the "best friend" that my parents were looking at private schools for me, the teasing became worse. I was called a snob and a rich girl behind my 41 back. The "best friend's" parents, even the father, whom I felt had a bit of compassion for me, found me ridiculous and called me neurotic to my face. I felt betrayed by them. They were the family I wanted to be a part of; they were a family together, while mine was falling apart. I don't think the "best friend's" parents were bad people. I just think I was a horse of another color that they didn't understand. I was different. I was a complicated girl in a very complicated situation, which made me even more complicated. They had their own kids and their own problems; they didn't need mine. They didn't know what to do with mine.

This high school hallway alienation / silent terrorism, however, became intolerable. Three or more girls huddled in a group is the high school equivalent of a sleeper cell and it is not to be fucked with. The devil is kinder. This hallway terror campaign began my downward spiral into hanging out with the "undesirables." I picked the stoners, the kids who smoked and drank, the promiscuous girls, and the kids from fucked-up families. If there was a kid with a problem, a bad family life or a kid with half a brain, I befriended them. With them I felt safe. With them, I felt like I was doing ok. I was, comparatively speaking. I liked them. They didn't judge me. They really didn't care about me one way or another. I just kind of moved along with them, merged into the crowd. I started hanging with the slut the "best friend" tortured. She was raised by her mom. Her dad was gone, not dead, just gone and she was nice to me. Nice to boys too. But she was no more of a slut than I was. Well, maybe a little. She was just a bit ahead of me in her search. I should have paid more attention to her slutiness. I might have saved myself a load of grief. But I was young and ageless. What did I know?

I think about her a lot. Because guess what? I actually liked her.

I also, surprise, surprise, met a boy in this crowd. He was three years older than me and drove. He protected me because his feelings for me were pure. He gave me a name. I was

42

"Kevin's Girlfriend". I went to a dress shop to find a prom dress. I thought he would ask me to go with him. I fell in love with myself, my newly named self with every dress I tried, twirling, twirling in the shops' mirror. I imagined me in my dress, on his arm, going to prom with a senior and the look of jealousy on the "best friend's" face. I never told my parents about this, never told Kevin.

Good thing.

He never asked me.

He did take me out to the neighborhood bars where he knew people so I wasn't carded. He took me places in his car, took me through the bases of teenage sexuality, took me so I wouldn't have to stay at home and see my father's decline. Took me away from myself and my fears of loneliness until he couldn't take me further because I wouldn't let him take me all the way.

He did take me through the transition from public high school to a most proper prep school in Connecticut.

That's where I ended up.

We looked at four schools: Choate, Taft, Canterbury and Kent. Choate was *really* moneyed and in the middle of the infamous 1980's "Choate Cocaine Bust." We were not sure that was the ideal place for me. Taft was the kind of place you forget you ever saw the minute you leave it. So, I can't say anything more about that. Canterbury seemed the choice for parents with somewhat spirited children; kids who were neither bad enough for The Berkshire School (which specialized in troubled youths when their parents had completely given up) nor did it have the qualifications to be titled one of the more "elite" prep schools. It served the parents bragging rights at a lowly country club. The name of the school kind of caught in their pseudo-lock-jawed throats. Lastly, there was Kent. It was the one place I adamantly refused to go to. I hated it on sight with the same passion I hated everything else in my life, except for Kevin.

Of course, Kent was where I went.

Out of the frying pan, right the hell into the fire.   43

My parents dropped me off next to an eight-foot high tower of Louis Vuitton luggage belonging to a Saudi Arabian princess and I knew I was sunk.

I knew I was sunk when I was left in a dorm room with a mousy girl who reminded me of a cute hamster. She had thick glasses, no interest in anything I was interested in and didn't seem too enthralled about me either. She did however have a wicked sense of humor and actually was very sweet. Comparatively speaking.

I knew I was sunk when the boys, face books in hand (a picture book of all new freshmen), sat on the boy's dormitory walls and studied possible new conquests the way a serial killer stalks his next victim.

I knew I was sunk when all the girls wore casual LL BEAN, LILLY PULITZER and LANDS' END like GUCCI and tossed their blond manes and blared their Crest whitened teeth, like for a snapshot whenever anyone called their names Muffy! Biffy! Bitsy!

I knew I was sunk when I spotted the throng in black, "Moon Pigs" they were called, a Goth-like minion, clad in dark thrift store overcoats, all looking like John Cusack in every film John Cusack has ever acted in, smelling of dank patchouli and clove cigarettes (I never could figure out how they stank so much of something that wasn't allowed on campus) and listening to Tears For Fears and The Cure.

I knew I was sunk when all the Prepsters played Hackey-Sack and listened to The Grateful Dead and canoodled together in a pack of tie-dyed poseurs in which I knew for a certainty as I knew back home that I would never fit.

Yet fit I tried. I couldn't find the stoners, smokers, or the drinkers because although they existed in the ivy-covered confine that was prep school, they weren't obvious. They couldn't be. Their $14,000.00 yearly tuitions Mommy and Daddy were handing out wouldn't permit their brazenness. I couldn't find the sluts either, because they basically all were and no one cared. After all, girls weren't just there to get a fine, expensive education. No. Girls were there for another, more important gain: rich, to the manor born husbands. No father in his right mind would tell his daughter to keep her skirt down when a young, very rich, very well familied, suitable prospective husband's hand was tugging it up around her head. Where to look? Where to look? Ah! There she is... the girl who is raised by her mother, dad gone, not dead, just gone, sent away to a Boarding School, which I assumed from conversation, was a far better alternative to living at home.

Enough said.

We became roommates.

I understood my attraction to her, but always wondered what she saw in me. Maybe it was my need to make her all right. My need to be her friend so she could in turn be, mine. She was a city girl with not much of anything in her pocket, but she was bright, pretty in an all-American jaunty sense and she was good with horses. I had more in my pocket, very bright in an all too commonly undiscovered way, pretty in an all too common undiscovered sense and was good with books and makeup. She would ride with abandon to escape and I would hide my mask of color into the calming lines of black and white and pray for change. In that sense we were the same: the flip sides of a coin. Whatever the reason we connected, I clung to her and she to me like two lifeboats gone amuck in a raging sea. Together we negotiated the prestige and found ourselves serving our time. She found the stoners, smokers and drinkers and I found the bitches.

There was this one girl. Short, plump, an athlete, I think. Played field hockey. A stupid sport if there ever was, dreamt up as the feminine equivalent of hockey so when girls were deigned admission into the hallowed grounds of prep schools they'd have an outlet for their viciousness. This girl had really beautiful blond hair. I mean beautiful; thick, swinging, long, gorgeous strands of gold. From afar she looked to be haloed. One morning, a crowd of teachers and students alike had gathered in the dining hall, around this girl whose hair had been savagely chopped off.

She was crying, holding her head and screaming, "Who did this? Who did this to me?!!!" You could hear her a mile away.

"WHO CUT MY HAIR WHILE I SLEPT LAST NIGHT!!!"

No one was ever caught and, of course, no one copped to it. But we all knew. In public school, the bitches taunt and leer, spread rumors and call names. Like I said, middle-class silent aggression. In prep school, it is OUT LOUD. These girls take what they want because they can. I steered pretty clear of these girls. They took love. Didn't give it. I needed it. I got it from my roommate, but she was onto more liquid pastures and so I found a senior who was as nice as nice could be.

She was a sweet one. Kris. But we called her Gils. Shortened from her last name. She was short, dark and beautiful to me. She was also an athlete. But mostly she was a gifted friend. I mean that in the sense that I have never, neither before nor since ever met anyone for whom friendship came so easily. She gave it freely and received it warmly. She became my paradigm for whom I wanted to be.

She taught me how to insert a tampon. She taught me how to talk to people and have them talk back to me. She taught me to have a sense of humor about myself, to not take myself so seriously. She taught me that Kent could be my saving grace. She brought me into her world. In her world of Saturday and Wednesday afternoon athletic games and Saturday night dances, I met her friends, who for some reason also ushered me into their worlds. I became the luckiest girl at Kent. All because of Gils, she of dark hair and fierce smile and laughter, decided I was to be saved.

I had, due to Gils, an ok sophomore year. I met a nice boy during my first few months' at Kent. Where is Kevin? You ask. Home, right where I needed him should I need his attention. He was my net in case I fell while trying to tiptoe the tightrope of prep-school popularity. This boy I met was a true good-ol'-boy from Texas. Daddy was in oil. He was Captain of the football team and just such a fucking gentleman. No rough-around-

46

the-edges-Long-Island-diner-out-of-a-Billy-Joel-song-Rat, to which I was accustomed. No, this boy, bless his heart, couldn't cause my heart to race unless he served me cup after cup of high-voltage espresso. Although he was the most popular sophomore, even dare I say, the most popular boy at Kent, he was destined to be just my friend. He was nice one at that; like a nice cup of cocoa. Warm, safe and inviting. What in hell was a Long Island girl going to do with that?

However lovely he was, he was not as good or as nice as Gils. No one ever could be. I had made a lasting friendship with Gils. Not so with my roommate. Not so for the roommates that came after her. Aside from my trunk full of bedding and books, my friendship with Gils was the single and only thing I brought out of Kent.

Upon her graduation in 1983, she took me with her to all the graduation parties. I was, I think the only sixteen year old. She took me with her to her parents' house on Martha's Vineyard, where she and her friends were celebrating their impending freedom in college.

It was a road trip. It was Gils, her sister, me, Andy, Lefty and Arnie among others. We drove from Connecticut to the Cape and from there took the ferry to the Vineyard. It was a fucking Carly Simon song. We got to her parent's house and the barrage of parties and drinking commenced like nobody's business. By day we hung on the beach, by night, well by night it was bacchanalia. I couldn't keep up with the lot of them, I was, remember, a few years their junior. I would fall asleep in one bed and by morning awake in another. I never really understood why or how that was until the end of the trip. Arnie, for whom I still have a soft spot, would carry me, in the wee hours of party dom, from the big bed in Gils' room into a small bed in one of the guest rooms. I was never the wiser.

It was Arnie carrying me in his arms and Gils directing his freight that taught me, during this week, the art of tenderness. Tenderness for a life not yet old enough to appreciate their fun and tenderness for a girl who without them would never have learned it at all. I recall that trip with Gils with great fondness.

It was the only time during those years I felt like I belonged. It was all because of Gils, she who welcomed me into her world and her family, she of fierce smile and laughter, decided I was to be saved.

That week went quick. The summer went quicker and back went I to Kent. Back to its ways, back to my roommates. This year we had a triple. First we had a "Diplobrat" (child of a Diplomat, just so you know) from South Africa. She spoke 14 languages and was bulimic. She would go into the bathroom, turn on all the faucets and puke her guts out in the bathroom stall. She didn't think anyone knew. *She spoke 14 different languages and didn't think anyone knew*. She was also a kleptomaniac. She stole other girl's underwear and shit. I never really knew. I never really knew *why*. By the time I could begin to figure it out, she was gone, not dead, just gone. The next girl was from Saudi Arabia. She was a piece of work. She used to write in her own menstrual blood on the walls: "GET ME OUT OF HERE! I HATE IT HERE!" It was fun. I liked her. This menophiliac had spunk. She got kicked out as well. I don't know why. That's prep school for you; one day a girl was there, the next…gone. Not dead, just gone.

Basquiat would have loved her; her menstrual blood art wasn't *that* offensive.

Either way, I moved on to…the common room.

It is hard to imagine boy/girl relationships within the confines of a prep school where our every movement is watched and documented by dorm heads, dining room heads, schoolhouse heads, teachers and other students alike. It is hard to understand how they even *exist* when the girl's campus is 4 and 1/2 miles up *hill* from that of the boys.

I have two, no rather three, no four, words for you.

Common room and hiking.

There were many a time I would get up in the middle of the night to pee only to find a boy or two doing the same in the girls' dorm bathroom! These horny boys would HIKE up the freaking hill at 2:30 in the morning. Just to get laid. I don't think I need the "just" in that previous sentence. The word "laid" is *justifying* enough. If they got caught, they were more than likely kicked out. Must have been mighty fine sex for such a risk, never mind the exercise.

Then there is the almighty common room. I don't mean the girls' common rooms. No. They were too bright, too airy, too open and too obvious. The boys' common room under the main dorm was dark and dank enough. It was there that the boy who got me to forget about Kevin (I was tired of the net. It's not a risk if you risk nothing) took me after lunch down at the boy's school for many a month. His name was Jason. He was fine. He was funny and smart. He was one of the born to the manor boys that girls fling themselves at. He was just dangerous enough to be sexy, yet kind enough to lure. He was perfect. He taught me many things on the two old and dusty, now-that-I-think-how-filthy-they-were-I-could-throw-up couches that were pushed together to make a makeshift bed. I am sure many a girl experienced her first orgasm on those couches. Ah, youth.

He taught me other things as well. He taught me how a boy can be unavailable and hurt a girl by withdrawing his affection just because he could. The more he withdrew, the more I hung on. The more I hung on the more it was over. The more it was over, the more I cried for my father. The more I cried for my father, the more alone I was.

I spent the remaining months of my junior year studying and reading my roommate's bloody graffiti.

I also ate a lot.

Enter Aiden. Aiden came to me in the summer of my junior year going into my senior year. I was fat. Gained the "freshman 15" so to speak. My mother told me to lose weight while I polished off the carton of Chocolate Häagen-Dazs that I took to eating during the school year and at home, standing in front of an open freezer. Ice cream and everything else put in front of me.

I joined our local gym and gained 210 lbs of Aiden.   49

I also lost about 165 pounds of Kevin, so really, if you think about it, I only really gained about 45 pounds of boy. Kevin took me as far as he could. He was good to me, nicer and more honest than I was to him. His was the first of a long line of nets strung together to protect my fall. I moved seemingly seamlessly, like a tightrope walking acrobat from one to the next.

Aiden was twenty-four to my seventeen. The "best friend's" parents now had even more to upbraid me about. They thought it ridiculous (they liked that word) and negligent of my parents to allow such a union. What they didn't know, couldn't know, is there but for the grace of God went they. Quite frankly there but for the grace of God went they about a lot of things. Judging is not parenting and parenting is not a contest to be won at the Country Club like a goddamned Limbo contest.

I think my parents condoned our relationship because they liked Aiden and knew he would take care of me. They knew he loved me. They knew he would visit me in prep school when they couldn't and entrusted my safety to him during those times they simply were too busy dealing with my father's illness to be present. They also knew Aiden took my virginity and although I don't think they were happy about that part, they knew it was going to happen one day, so why not with Aiden, who for all intents and purposes took care of me when they, my parents, couldn't.

Blessed Aiden was there for me during my last year of Kent, which was the hardest. All of my friends had graduated and I was alone with psychotic vampire roommates and a family skating on really thin ice. What time I didn't spend in the library or in the new "upper classmen common room" -- not to be confused with the "porno common room"—I spent on the phone to Aiden. I called him every second I could, every lunch break, every pee break. I am sure my parents' phone bill, because I had a calling card that was attached to their account, was astro-fucking-nominal. I existed only for the weekends when either Aiden or I would travel the two hours to be together. Considering students were only allowed two weekends a year off campus, not including holidays and summer break, Aiden did most of the traveling. My parents had put him on the list of people allowed to take me off campus. I suspect they knew exactly what we did on these furlongs. I suspect the head master and teachers knew as well. They also knew that if these outings were to be forbidden, I would take myself out of Kent, marry Aiden on the sly, get knocked up and run off to God knows where.

My Dorm Mother made a deal with me. If I took on the job as Dorm Head, (making sure bathrooms and common rooms were clean and girls were in bed at lights-out) she would let me use the phone to call Aiden after lights-out. I took the deal. I was given this leniency like a gift. I was given freedom other students did not have. It wasn't that I was a great asset to Kent. I wasn't a star athlete or a star student, but I was something to them. Broken perhaps. I think they knew even more than my parents that without access to Aiden, I would deteriorate. Quickly.

No one wanted that on his or her heads. I never abused the freedom and trust they instilled in me, but I did what I wanted, when I wanted. What my teachers saw when they looked at me, was a girl holding on tight. The rope I hung onto would either hang me or tether me. They were betting on the tethering.

I remember telling my mother at graduation that graduating from Kent would be the most important day of my life. Nothing would ever compare to it. No bell to sound the end of rounds, I just kept fighting my way through a place where someone like me never should have been in the first place. I fought hard to stay there, to do well and make my family, my father proud. I fought against the norm, against the standards of the quintessential New England Prep School and upon holding that rolled up parchment in my sweaty little hand I knew I had won. I figured if I could get through the three years of Kent I could get through anything.   51

In a certain sense, I was right... Those three years prepared me for a lot. They prepared me for New York University, for one thing. But what I didn't expect, what I could not anticipate was the constant state of panic I lived in during my four years of college.

*****

Aiden and I had broken up. My father called it when he said I couldn't be mad at the man for outgrowing him. We had picked out a ring or at least the type of ring I wanted and I had accepted his proposal without him properly proposing. I knew shortly after that I had made a terrible mistake. I had an epiphany of sorts. I saw myself ten years down the road with Aiden and what I saw I didn't care for: living in Upstate New York in the freezing cold, outside a dilapidated body builders gym that we owned and pregnant with our fifth kid. This was a vision of a life that I knew would swallow me whole, douse my fire and bury me deep. I ended our relationship, cut up the net and five months later heard Aiden married an aerobics instructor. They found fitness and health together. I found emptiness and despair alone. That breakup was the beginning of my panic. I felt abandoned by myself. I chose me and ended up with nothing. Everything around me seemed to be dying and I became terrifically unglued.

Ironically and poetically, this was also the period in my life where acting found me. I was a sure bet, a perfect target: pretty, angry, emotionally volatile, highly dramatic, intense and just aching to be someone else. If I am honest, I was born an actress. Seeing The *Turning Point* with Anne Bancroft and Shirley Maclaine when I was about ten years old and later finding out acting was also my father's dream just sealed the deal. Rachel Ward in *Sharkey's Machine* did nothing to dissuade me...she was and is the bomb and I wanted to be just like her. But acting wasn't something I considered or even thought of at prep school or the first two years of NYU. It just kind of happened *to* me. So it must have been providential. In any event, during this early time in my career, I was received well and given a pass so to speak, an artistic license to be fucked-up. My behavior could easily be dismissed with "Oh, she's an actress." But I couldn't dismiss it. Acting helped, but it was no cure for that which ailed me.

I was a literal poster child for any number of panic disorders. I was the perfect personification of ANXIETY. I doctor shopped during this time like most college kids rushed fraternities. In my sophomore year I was convinced I had AIDS. Then I was sure I had cancer; prostate cancer to be exact. All that money for private education and I didn't know women don't have a prostate. I suffered with intestinal problems, ulcers, Hiatal Hernias and Irritable Bowel Syndrome.

I lived in constant fear of everything. Dying. Disease. My school classes, nightclubs, people, certain food groups and all beverages except for cranberry juice had the potential to send me in a downward spiral of anxiety bordering on the psychotic. I also counted. I counted the number of steps from my apartment building to my classroom chair. If I was off by just one step, or if someone else were sitting in my chosen "safe" chair, I would count the steps back home. I counted steps to subway stations, dining halls, my friend's dorms or apartments. I counted everything but couldn't count on myself.

If I had an attack with a particular person, I would never see that person again. If I had an attack after eating or drinking something, I would never eat or drink that thing again. If I went to a restaurant as there were three or four I allowed myself to go to, I needed to sit as close to an exit as possible yet have full view of the kitchen or bar area so I could watch the preparation of my order. I feared large crowds of people for fear of being stuck by random hypodermic needles.

I feared all boys I dated as being hosts to a myriad of diseases that could harm and kill me.

I would never shake hands.

I was a mess.

No doctor ever diagnosed me as having anything   53

serious.

I had become a master at hiding my symptoms even from them.

I was, after all, an actress.

Nevertheless, my coping machinations became so sophisticated that even my own mind did not know what my body surely did: that I was indeed coping.

I saw a timeline that became my whole existences through-line: the day my father was diagnosed with brain cancer was the day I had my first encounter with palpable fear. Never having dealt with it or spoken to anyone about it at twelve years of age, I was living the consequences at twenty and beyond. That was hard to do when I was young and ageless and doomed to be emotionally twelve for the rest of my adult life. They say (I'm not sure who the "they" is) that an alcoholic remains the same age emotionally as when they first start drinking. I say a person remains the same age emotionally as when their parent begins to die. So, I am still twelve. In my heart and in my spirit, but not around my eyes or my tummy (three kids you know.)

My ass though? Still nice and high.

I remember going to the Catholic Church on East 12th St. one afternoon. I felt the need to talk to a priest. I *needed* to talk to a priest. I walked up the church steps to open the door and found it chained and padlocked. I stared dumbfounded. The one time I went to church on my fucking own without prodding from the old Catholic Italian ladies in my family, the one time I actually NEEDED to speak to a servant of our Lord and the fucking door was LOCKED? I sat on the steps in complete confusion and I cried.

How apro-fucking-pos. I couldn't deal anymore. I didn't understand what my body was attempting to tell me with these anxious, tearful moments that were occurring more and more.

How was I to know that every attack, every anxious moment and every gasp of air that gave power to a new and fresh sob, was a cry of grief?

It was grief. Just that and that alone.

Grief for a father I loved and adored. Who was *gone*, not dead, just *gone*, but whom I was deadly aware was dying.

Grief for a teenage girl who never really got to enjoy and live because I had existed only to worry about my father's illness.

Grief for the young woman I was fast becoming who I couldn't hear and hardly ever acknowledged.

I think I panicked for all the goddamned "mes" that were forgotten in my pursuit to forget all the circumstances that made me me.

That was college, in a nutshell. I spent the four years of college panicking in advance, just in case I didn't have time in the future, for the five months that began in August 1990.

Chapter Four

"I wanted God. In Heaven and on earth I sought,
And lo! I found him in my inmost thought."

I Wanted God
Kate Chopin[2]

AUGUST 1990

"Your father says he's been speaking to God."

My mother told me this over our morning coffee. My brother was at college in Vermont, so only I was privy to this. It was their first day home from the hospital in Philadelphia. My father watched me and spoke for the first time in six months.

"No more treatments. God says no more treatments."

Ten years ago he had a brain tumor. Now it's Lymphoma. A brain tumor is forthcoming and easy to detect. Lymphoma is like a ghost haunting dark hallways playing a very short game of hide and seek. It may not always be visible on the numerous CAT scans and MRIs he's had, but it has certainly left its imprint.

I didn't know what to expect when I saw him. Because I had been in school and he in hospitals, I had not seen him for about a month. Would he be completely bald? Had he regained feeling on his right side? Could he maybe take a few steps on his own? Did the Chemo work at all? Would he know my name?

It had been six months since he spoke coherently. His tumor, located in the upper left lobe of his brain hit a spot that impedes speech. Aphasia - "The partial or total loss of speech or the understanding of language." Even more horrific was that my father's lucidity was never challenged or in any way impaired, which made his inability to articulate his thoughts more tragic. He was also paralyzed on his right side. When this began to manifest, dad called it the "condom thing." He said he felt like he had a condom on his hand, like he knew he was touching a table but couldn't feel its texture. Only by sight did he know what he was touching. Gradually the "condom thing" engulfed his entire right side. Thank God it isn't his left side.

He's a lefty, a southpaw.

*****

Mom called from the garage, needing help to get Dad into the house. Although weak from the treatment, with his walker and leg brace he managed a few baby steps. The rest of the way mom and I carried him.

It made me sick. It made me angry. It made me dizzy with a compassion I have never before felt. Guilty of cowardice or self-preservation, I simply could not imagine his feelings at being carried by two women. Not even two years before, this 6 ft. 175 lb. man carried us. He looked at me...as if reading my mind and the helplessness loss of pride and honor wept from his eyes in apology.

We made it into the kitchen. I had spent hours prior to their arrival cleaning the house and making Dad's favorite lunch: tuna fish sandwiches with diced dill pickles, mustard and potato chips. He was always hungry. The steroids he was taking to control the swelling in his brain leave him voracious. However humble our feast, it wasn't hospital food and he ate and ate until all was finished and he was covered in a fine dusting of potato chip crumbs. We laughed.

It had been a long time since that sound was made or heard in our house.

He had to use the bathroom. We were limited in our choice of bathrooms as two were too far away in the house to carry him to and the closest in the kitchen was too small to accommodate the three of us. Mom helped him off with his pants and slipped a bedpan beneath him right at the kitchen table. I never thought I'd see any kitchen table used in this way, especially ours. It gave new meaning to the cliché, "Don't shit

58

where you eat."

Cancer may not allow dignity but we did, so we left him there in privacy. Not two minutes passed and we heard a loud crashing thud from the den. Hurdling the couch and running into the kitchen we found him, face down, arms flailing at his sides, naked from the waist down, lying in his own shit. It was everywhere. The floor, the walls, the table, the chairs, everything was covered. He'd had a seizure.

"Oh God, Matt, don't die now. NO! Not like this. Please God not like THIS!"

Over and over my mother wept this mantra.

"Schmoo? Can you hear me? JESUS FUCKING CHRIST CAN YOU HEAR ME?"

I ran out of the house. I ran to find some help. Across the street was a family with five sons. No one home. Next door was another family with...I stopped cold. I knew my mother would not want anyone to see our family this way and I knew my father wouldn't want anyone to see him this way. For they would see what I saw as I walked back through our front door... my father's eyes rolling back into his head. The whites shimmering with rage at his illness and fear of what he knew but could no longer say. They would hear what I heard. The death rattle harmonizing with my mothers sobs. They might do as I did. Turn my back on the bare-assed, white-eyed, gasping monster that was my father.

I called George. He was the older brother of one of my childhood schoolmates. He was the black sheep of his family. He was strange, soft-spoken and oddly childlike for a man of his strength, height and age. He had a weird fascination with Prince and apparently had his own problems with drugs and alcohol. That's why we hired him. My friend said his brother needed a job and we met with him. He was quiet and possessed a strength of compassion I had never seen in another human being. He was not an extremely bright man. But he was a kind man, a man of character and honor. He also told us we were mixing dad's meds wrong. You want to know about drugs? You go to three people: Pharmacist, Dealer or 59

User. We agreed to try the drug cocktail his way and hired him on the spot.

My mother was trying to hold up two businesses, I was trying to audition and Matt, my brother, was at college at University of Vermont. Someone always had to be with my father and we were struggling to balance our "life goes on" schedules with his "life may be ending very soon" schedule and we needed help: a nanny, a sitter, another set of strong hands.

After I called him, George dropped everything he was doing and drove over. He only lived a few streets down, but in his way of always being there it seemed like the second I hung up the phone there he was in our doorway.

"Hey Matt. Had a tough one, huh. Not to worry Big Man. Let's get you cleaned up." George said.

He carried my father into the big bathroom and because he couldn't hold my father up in the shower, got into the bath with him. He sat in my father's dirty water and bathed him clean. He toweled my dad off, dressed him and carried him to bed and sat there with him. Quietly sat there. They didn't speak. He just sat while my father closed his eyes not wanting to look at the boy/man who just bathed him like a baby. George patted my dad's hand.

"Not to worry Big Man, not to worry." George whispered.

I fell in love with him then and there.

George came over every day after that regardless of whether my mother or I were there. He sat with my father. Fed him, cleaned him, drugged him up, down and zigzag. He carried him into the pool and held him as the water flowed over his body. George took him to his family's beach club for lunch and to look at the boats coming in with tired water skiers and partiers and fishing rigs delivering their daily catch. It was a strange coupling made fine by the sheer fact that both my father and George were giving so much to each other. George cared for my father and my father gave George something, someone to care about.

Until I stepped in.

60   I said I fell in love with him and I did. We spent a lot of

time together, George and I, caring for my father. We spent a lot of time together, just George and I. Mostly we fooled around. I knew he was no match for me intellectually and he knew that too. I knew he was not husband material for me and he knew that too. I knew he needed a family to give a shit about him the same way I needed someone to give a shit about me and we did that together, mostly in the back seat of a car in the parking lot of the beach club his family belonged to. Sometimes we went out to drink. The bartenders in my hometown, of which there were plenty, all remembered me from Kevin, so although I had just become legal, I'd been in their bars so long, they all thought I was a seasoned fixture. Mostly, they probably just humored me, knowing as all small town barkeeps do who needs a goddamned drink.

I was back in the group of the "best friend" and this union of mine, George and I, only added to the image they had made of me years prior -- that I was out of my mind. I had come out of Kent, NYU and the "City," an "Actress" and dating-no colliding with someone whom they considered beneath them.

I am sure the group's parents had a fucking field day. Apparently, I was still the subject of coffee talk for many a bored mother, like my own young adult version of a tabloid!

But again, they didn't know what I knew. They couldn't know what I knew. There but for the grace of God... Their "town loser" was my family's angel. He was a fucking angel and they all were blessed to be in his presence.

George, like Kevin, took me places, bars, the beach the back seat of our cars where we rounded the bases, never going home. I think he was just as confused by our coupling as I was, as everyone else was. Mostly, I think he was happy to have someone who found his special qualities, special. Also, because he told me what he really wanted to be was a priest.

Who was I to ruin his dream?

Chapter Five

"Don't tell yourself its never going to end.
And, don't fall upon the blade of your own pain.
Just keep breathing in and breathing out
And breathing in and breathing out…"

"My Unusual Day"
Ned Farr

LATE AUGUST 1990

"Mom, Daddy won't wake up. He says, or rather motions, arm slicing through the air like an Ump calling SAFE, that he doesn't want to get up, he doesn't want to eat." I say this to my mother as I walk in to the kitchen for dinner.

Panic has set in. The inevitable has dawned: withdrawal from the External World. This is one of the first of the last stages of life and can last throughout the process. During this time, it could be days or hours before death, the dying sleep more and more toward their end. This is the beginning of letting go of life and the preparing for death. Food is a burden, chewing is exhaustive, weakness becomes paralyzing and what once was a bed is now a makeshift coffin simply awaiting burial. Dad is sleeping 18 out of the 24 hours in a day. Coma is imminent. Death is just around the corner.

We ate dinner alone, Mom and I. George goes home to give us privacy during these meals. They weren't enticing enough for him to stay. These meals usually consist of a Xanax and a half, no fuck it, a full bottle of wine for Mom and a glass, no fuck it, 3 glasses of wine for me and maybe a few bites of whatever. The Caregiver's Diet. You'll shed those pesky extra 10-20, but not so much fun.

We went into the bedroom afterwards. Dad was sitting up! On his own! He had, we didn't know how, taken off his pants and was trying to get out of bed.

"Where are you going?" My mother asked him.

He pointed at nothing in particular, miraculously stood up on his own, took a few feeble steps and fell. Mom, all 98 pounds of her, somehow caught and balanced him. She under his right arm and I under his left, walked around the house for quite some time. Finally he stopped and deep in thought, he began to mumble.

"Daddy, we can't hold you up any longer. Let me go and get the wheel chair."

"One more." He said as he sat.

"One more what?" We asked.

"One more day." He repeated.

"One more day and what Schmoo?" My mother asked.

"One more day." Again SAFE with the arm.

"Go away." He said.

"Is it time, Matt? Do you want me to call Matthew home?" My mother asked him nervously, knowing the answer.

"Yes. My son. One more day." SAFE.

Let's see...

Dad had thus far lived to see Matthew's graduation from Kent in May. Yes, he went there too. He was a perfect Kentie: Schoolhouse Head, Soccer Captain, Lacrosse Captain, Squash Captain and Tennis Captain. The deep, poetically dark, Ally Sheedy in *Breakfast Club* image I had worked so hard on at Kent was shattered.

Damn him.

More recently, Dad lived to see my graduation from NYU. After the former, we had gathered at a local Italian restaurant in Huntington where Dad promptly fell in the parking lot trying to get out of the car. He was wearing a cream linen suit, looking much like John Gotti would had his son just been released not from prison, but from the ivied tentacles of an exclusive New England Prep School. His knees were bloodied and the stains were obvious. We managed to walk into the restaurant and to our table. In passing, I heard some country club, lock-jawed bitch bellow at the top of her faux blond, anorexic lungs "You'd think people would have heard of dry-cleaning." I literally had to be restrained. My brother held me back and the woman, suitably frightened, shut the fuck up.

Nice.

The later cause for celebration was one month later. It was held in my apartment in New York's most chic Lower East side where dodging bullets was soon to become an Olympic sport. I shared this fashionable address with a girlfriend, whose brother I worked for. I managed the books and worked the door of his very hot nightclub in Greenwich Village, in between auditions, acting jobs and trying to graduate on time from college. Their mother very kindly wanted to have a party for me.

The radio was playing Sinead O'Conner's "Nothing Compares 2 U" and my father asked me to dance. Around and around we circled and I became aware that every set of eyes was on us. He stared at me and scratched his chin and out came a clump of his beard. He kissed me sheepishly and whispered "hair of the dog that bit you." It was funny and sad, but that was indicative of my father...humor in the face of sadness.

We were pretty sure Dad would not make it to see Matthew graduate from UVM. We were pretty sure Matthew wouldn't make it to graduate from UVM. Since my father had been on the decline since 1989, Matthew had been pulled out of school more than he'd even been there. So the phone call, once again, had to be made.

Before we called, Dad had to use the bathroom. Mom knelt beside him and whispered.

"You'll be free, Matt. Free. It's what you wanted. It's what you told me last week in the hospital."

Before they had come home to my tuna fish sandwiches and potato chip lunch, my father told her they had one more week together. Starting Wednesday. My mother did all she could to get him released but his white blood count was too high. The doctors told her that taking him home would greatly increase his chance of getting an infection, like a cold, which would kill him.

We should be so lucky. (Later in the fall, we did bring him outside when it was really cold. We all got bronchitis. He was fit as a fiddle.)

Wednesday passed for them, Thursday then Friday. My father was slipping deeper into depression when finally my mother had enough and getting the release forms and a pen from the nurse, handed them to my father who, she said, signed them "fuck you."

We put him into bed. He slept. We made phone calls. Matthew was coming home on the weekend.

Chapter Six

"You know the time will come my dancin' boy
When you're dancin' days are done,
And when daddy and his dancin' boy
Will have dwindled down to one."

"Dancin' Boy"
Harry Chapin

SEPTEMBER 1990

"Kids!" It echoed through the house and I wasn't sure if I was dreaming. It is 5 AM on Saturday morning. I swam up from sleep to hear it again.

"Kids! NOW!" The echo had a name. Mom.

Matthew and I collided in the hallway outside our bedrooms and found Mom holding our father up on his feet. He wanted to go for a walk. We slept walked him back to bed.

"This is what I came home for? This is what you two have been dealing with? I'm not going back. I am not going back," Matthew loudly hissed to me.

Having said his peace, Matthew went back to his room and shut his door.

I left. Didn't know or care where I was going, I just left.

I drove around a bit. I don't remember how long I was in the car, but it must have been awhile because I got hungry. So I went to get frozen yogurt at the new place where they mix candy and cookies and stuff into it. Afterwards, I pulled out into traffic, made a U-turn and got hit. It was so appropriate to the day. It was appropriate that it was my father's car, the piece of shit Mercedes I used to threaten to leave on the side of the road it was that much of a lemon.

I came back to a few hours later to find my mother

hysterical trying to reach the doctor. I figured news of the car could wait, but she saw it outside in the driveway from the window and proceeded to have a nervous breakdown.

"GOD DAMN IT" She screamed at me. "You think that was what I needed today? You are paying for that! And now I can't wake your father. He's not responding to me. See if you can get him up."

I went into their room. He was sleeping. I called his names.

"Daddy. Matt." Nothing. I sprinkled water on his face. Nothing. I broke the ammonia sticks the hospice nurse left us for this very reason and nothing. Finally, I hauled off and slapped his face. Nothing.

The doctor finally called back only to say, "Well, he's probably just hemorrhaging in his brain."

Thank God it was nothing serious.

Whatever. My father was in a coma.

The paramedics came.

Mom went with them. I stayed home to wait for Matthew who went out with his girlfriend. We'd given George some much deserved time off since we now had an extra set of hands. So I just sat and waited in my house alone. It was different. Being there alone. Not that I'd never been alone before, but there was no sound. No people. No commotion. No nothing. I thought maybe this is what my father's end is like. Quiet. Engulfed in nothingness. It was nice. But I wanted to fill the silence, offer myself some memories and exorcize the demons …so I played the piano. I often played along, be it on the piano or my flute to my dad's 8-track Cassettes. He was a big music buff, especially jazz. He loved all of it. My uncle is a jazz pianist and lore has it, as a child, I was once held by the great and elegant Lena Horne. I played by ear to Al Jarreau, Oscar Peterson, Qincy Jones, Manhattan Transfer, Cleo Laine and then later to Billy Joel, Carly Simon and Harry Chapin.

I played music a lot hoping my father would hear me.

Hearing is apparently the last sense to leave a person.

I always assumed Dad could hear me even when he was asleep. I wanted him to feel like he's still here, still a part of our lives, part of the hullabaloo and noise of the living.

Today I also played my flute. I played Chuck Mangione's *Consuelo's Love Theme*. It was one of my dad's favorites. I thought perhaps my notes could reach him at Huntington Hospital and he would know I was thinking of him. I wielded my flute like a weapon, like a musical divining rod leading me to the point of origin of the evil that needed to be exorcised from our house. It led me into every room of the house. I hunted the cancer, I hunted the misery it had caused and ended up almost beating the hell out of Matthew's girlfriend who had walked in the back door. Matthew was behind her and finding my exorcism by woodwind fruitless, we left for the hospital.

In his car. The Mercedes as I said…not in good condition.

My father was given a chest exam and a CAT scan to determine if, in fact, there was any bleeding in his brain. Throughout, he remained unconscious. There was no bleeding. The doctor was wrong. There was, however, a large mass of tumors and an incredible amount of edema. The swelling was taking over his brain and there was nothing anyone could do.

His brain was drowning.

We were called, Matthew, our mother and I into a room to confer with the doctor.

It was a small room with light blue walls. It was a claustrophobic's nightmare. We crammed in, the three of us and the doctor conferred.

"Wouldn't the steroids bring down the swelling?" We asked.

"With the amount he's already on, if that didn't stop it, nothing will. You have two choices: take him off the steroids and let nature take his course or keep him on, reduce the swelling and prolong his life."

This was the doctors' sage advice.

Okay.

70 Somebody must have confused us with God.

Huge mistake.

The answer became very clear to us and hinged solely on one very important question.

Prolong *what* life?

*****

We waited. We waited. We waited for him to die.

No tears. We searched each other's faces as if expecting to suddenly see the face of God to alleviate our anxiety and saw only familial resemblance. I saw our family doctor, the one we went to for our yearly physicals, in the hallway. I told her I wasn't feeling well and that perhaps I was coming down with something bad, like Strep throat or the flu. I made her feel my glands and look in my throat. She was patient and kind and told me that stress could do very bad things to otherwise very healthy people. There was, she said, nothing wrong with me other than that my father was in a coma and dying and I could do nothing about it. She said it was one of the saddest things she ever saw and that if I needed anything to please call her.

I *was* calling. She wasn't picking up. I needed, though what I needed I didn't know.

My father was unconscious for six hours.

He woke up.

We didn't expect this.

He asked for … Burger King.

If it had existed then, he would have Super-Sized it.

We drove to the drive-thru. Ordered. Brought it home and feasted. The Governor had made the call. We were reprieved. We just ate our food. No one said much. We three knew what we had done. We had condemned Dad before all the evidence was in. We were jury, judge and executioner before we heard both closings. We were ashamed. We were shameful. Shame on us. We tortured ourselves with questions: Did we do the right thing? Did we make the right decision? He just ate a super-sized meal of a Whopper and fries from

Burger King, goddamn it! The dying are very tricky, slippery folk. They like to play parlor tricks with your psyche. What we thought was his miraculous recovery was in fact just a window of lucidity for him and a window of opportunity for us to go madhouse crazy. The questions were endless and unanswerable. We did, in the end, what we thought he'd want. He told us that first day home, "God said no more treatments." He said "No more, final say." We believed him. I don't know if he knew what we had done, the awful choice we had made.

I don't know if he knew. I'll always wonder.

Our lives were woven together in a familial blanket of functional dysfunction. Like conjoined quadruplets sharing one heart, what one felt, we all felt. Like some macabre ballet, we danced around each other, knowing our roles, playing our parts, surrounding the nucleus that was my father's cancer. In its cruelty and ugliness there was a brutal beauty, for it brought us together in the selflessness of care giving.

Our ballet had an audience. It was here that I learned a very important lesson. Where audiences are concerned very few are worth the art they view. We had a constant flow of visitors during this time, at the hospital and at our house. Family and friends. Some were supportive. Most were cowardly fools who thought if they got too close they could catch it as if brain cancer was spreading through the neighborhood like a bad case of head lice.

People cried a lot.

I realized they didn't cry for my father. If they did, they would have done so in private. They cried for themselves. They cried in fear and horror that what they saw, when they look at my father, could one day be the mirror image of them. So they cried in public, for who would be there to console their visceral fear in private? We were left to coddle the weak and stroke the selfish while staring into the eyes of a man frightened by the tears he saw shimmering in the eyes of others.

The lesson learned: don't cry in front of the dying. All that does is scare them. The same goes for out of town visitors.

Because these past days had been hard, my grandfather came up from North Carolina. Upon seeing him, my father began sobbing. Not because he was glad to see my grandfather, there was no love lost there, but because he knew it must be terribly bad and that his time must be running out for my grandfather, who never liked my father in the first place, to come and see him.

The barrier of strength we had worked so hard to uphold was shattered by the crying and the visitors.

Made our job of smiling through the pain that much harder.

I called my friend Ned. Ned was and still is a friend from my NYU days. A musician I met, who was a friend of a musician I once dated. I think I collected boyfriends like some women collect shoes. Which one I picked depended on my outfit or mood as it were. Ned fit my mood. Ned fit any mood really, he was a moody, dreamy guy made all the more sexy by a microphone kissing his lips as he strummed his guitar...killed me softly, I think it goes. I would often during this time take the train into the city. Ned and I would meet up with a few of our mutual friends. Sometimes we would go to the gig of another musician we knew and sometimes we would just go to his apartment and fool around. Around the bases, never going home. It was a sexual and emotionally deviant collision course. I didn't *date* men. I collided with them. Man, was I searching. Searching for man. I went to keep up my friendships. I went to clear my head. I went to get the fuck out of my house. I went to feel another's hands on my body, to feel if I *could* feel. To hear voices that didn't belong to my family, to hear noise that wasn't scary and I went to be normal. I went to *feel* normal. I stood at Huntington Train Station in hopes, in need, for the train heading west, to take me away from the death of the east.

Go west, go west, go west.

This time he came east.

He came out to the Island. I took him to Caumsett State Park. It's a huge mansion on beautiful grounds on the causeway in Lloyd Neck, Long Island. It is on 1900 acres of   73 the old Marshall Field estate. The leaves were changing and it had started to get a little cold and we went just as dusk was approaching. We walked the entire park, chatting lightly about our lives, catching up with friends through each other. We finally found ourselves in a secluded little overhang onto the Long Island Sound. It was growing dark and there was a fine mist that hung about us and in front of us was just the most beautiful expanse of blue and gray. We hung, suspended in the smokiness that seemed to reach out to us from the water and engulf us in a cool, wet embrace. I felt like I was being hugged by God. I felt that if I just put one more foot in front of the other, the heavy haze would hold my weight and carry me into the blue and gray where I could wait for my father and guide him home.

I wanted to leap into it. I wanted a wave to swell and sweep me into the curve of its curl and go home. I wanted to stay in this overhang, protected by the branches hanging down from the trees that secluded it and stare into the water forever. Ned felt the same way, because I remember he stopped talking. He took my hand and he stopped talking.

We waited for the sun to completely disappear and we walked, Ned and I, back to my car, our way lit only by the embers of the cigarette I had just lit.

*****

Mom had to tie up some loose ends at work. During this time she was in the process of selling her home health care company, Breath of Life, and closing down my father's photography studio. She had sold all the photography equipment to my father's photographer and was just tiding up everything else. Matthew and I had to take dad for his blood tests.

As soon as we got him in to the car, he decided he wanted to go for a drive. He couldn't tell us exactly where he wanted to go, but we knew he had something specific in mind as he kept shaking or nodding his head at every turn we made heading home. Somehow he managed to say beach and the beach was where we took him. We drove to the beach where he had spent much of his youth. We sat silent in the car watching our father watch everything around him. I think I heard the shutter click in his heart, taking pictures of his beach. There he is as a boy with this father flying the kites my grandfather so loved. There he is with his brother, my Uncle Anthony, playing one last football game before their numbers were called for the Vietnam Draft. There he is on his moped, driving to see my mother who had just returned from Europe where she sang with her college choir. There he is with my mother, a lovely diamond glistening on her left hand. There they are together walking down the aisle after the priest has announced them husband and wife.

There he is holding his infant daughter, then teaching his little girl how to swim. Another, playing sand soccer with his son, at two years old, five, thirteen, sixteen, and at eighteen. Shutter speed like lightning. CLICK. CLICK. CLICK. CLICK. CLICK. CLICK. CLICK. CLICK. CLICK. CLICK. CLICK. CLICK...Ad infinitum.

As soon as we pulled into the garage, Dad had to use the bathroom. We moved as fast as we could, but only got as far as the little kitchen bathroom. It was too small. He had an accident. Poor Father. I wondered if he wondered if that would be the image we remembered. We carried him into this room, washed, changed him and laid him down to rest. We then went back into the kitchen to clean up the mess. We said nothing to each other. There wasn't anything to say.

*****

My father says God will take him formally.

He told me the feeling he has now is faith. He has never felt that before.

He also told me four of his childhood friends were sitting with him at the foot of the bed.

He said they came for a visit.

He talks of the man with the hard hair and the blue   75

lady with the blue hair as he points toward heaven.

He heaves his body upward and cries "JESUS. JESUS. TAKE ME."

The blue lady with the blue hair hovers over him and we see his lips move wordlessly, whispering to her as if in prayer but opening wider to scream. JESUS. JESUS. Pointing upward.

Always pointing upward.

I found this interesting.

He can't find words to express his everyday needs, but can summon them to express religious dogma and visitations from beyond with such conviction and eloquence. There must be some providential force behind these words coming from his aphasiac mouth: JESUS, JESUS, JESUS. He is turning to the "other world" now. He is talking to old friends and family members. He is at the gate and they are all welcoming him. He sees them standing around his bed, waving to him to come through, to cross over, and to join them. "Oh! The places he'll go, the things he'll see," says Dr. Seuss! They whisper the secrets my father will soon come to know. The knowledge he had to forget all those years ago when he traveled through my grandmother and left God. I feel it.

But, shall I believe? Shall I pray? Shall I...?

Ourladyfullofgracethebluelladywiththebluehairthelord iswiththeetakemyfatherblessedartthouamongwomentakemy fatherblessedisthefruitofthywombjesusChristTAKEMYFATHER.

Chapter Seven

"To the actress,
Who strives or dreams
Whether at liberty or stardom
Taking on her own life
And, the lives of others,
Offering magic
Pretending miracles."

Anonymous[3]

OCTOBER 1990

    I went into my father's room.
    I have an audition today. It's a good script. The character is perfect. I've studied hard and I think I can do it.
    "Dad? Dad? I'm going to get this job for you."
    Stupid.
    He touched my face.
    Go west. Go west. On the train I thought how wonderful it would be to get a really great film that I auditioned for on the ten-year anniversary of my father's battle with cancer.
    I thought it poetic justice.
    Like I said before, my father was one of the reasons I became an actress. When he was in his early twenties it was what he wanted to do. That and become a doctor. He was smart. He had a back up plan. But, at the time, his family couldn't afford medical school and he had had a very providential conversation one night after he and my mother announced their engagement. They were at the Crescent Club where my grandfather had been president for twenty-five years. A doctor friend of my grandfather had been told my father wanted to go to medical school. Upon hearing about all the different schools and scholarships my father had applied for he asked a very simple yet defining question within their parley.
    "Could you tell your wife, mother, father, child, they were

78

dying?" He asked.

"I'll have to think about that." My father replied.

He did.

He couldn't.

No more backup plan.

When I read the pre-canon books my parents filled out prior to getting married, I learned that my father's greatest dream was to be a contract player on a soap opera. I loved that. He never said he wanted to be Montgomery Clift and by the way, he could have been, they were twins, except I think my dad was more handsome. He never said he wanted to be a Broadway star or Alan Alda. He just wanted to be on a soap opera.

Anyway, I came along and although he kept his toes wet by modeling and doing industrials and regional commercials, he went to work, willingly yet numbly, for my grandfather.

This was obviously not my father's choice of career, but it was a necessary one. As I have stated before, there was no love lost between my maternal grandfather and my father. I think my grandfather saw my father as the son of a poor, blue-collar, house-painting, bus-driving immigrant. I think he thought my mother had married beneath her. But my mother loved my father with all her heart and since he could not change that, my grandfather gave him a job. My grandfather owned a welding supply company that supplied companies like Grumman. He made my father the vice president of the company and made his own son, who was, so I am told, less deserving, president. "Blood is blood," my grandfather had said.

My father was brilliant with people. He was incredibly important to the company because of this. People called my father for whatever they needed, bypassing my uncle and grandfather. He was the good soldier. He never asked for any credit for this and apparently never received any. He was under-appreciated and I have heard the word "abused" to describe his treatment at this company. My grandfather was having an affair with his secretary. Everyone knew, except my mother. My father covered for my grandfather. He kept it 79 from my mother because he knew how hurt she would be and because, apparently, that was part of his job.

Ironic. I think the rejection that is par for the course as an actor might have been kinder.

However, the sperm that carried me would have the last laugh. I shot out of him an actress. I was ready for my close-up the second it burrowed within my mother's egg.

I kept the dream alive. He saw in me a chip off the ol' block. In my junior year of NYU I told my parents that I had been signed by the ELITE modeling agency and that I wanted to be an actress. My mother told me to empty my pockets, my father beamed. My education had cost them hundreds of thousands of dollars and I was about to piss away the whole lot of it. My mother was softly enraged. My father could not have been more gleeful.

I modeled, got myself an agent and manager and my father was THRILLED.

When I got my first gig as Hostess of MTV's *Remote Control* my father was in the hospital getting chemotherapy. Weeks later, after we began taping the show, he was back in with phlebitis in his leg. I brought him a tape of one of the shows. I also brought Colin Quinn, Ken Ober the hosts of *Remote Control*, one of the producers of the show and my college girlfriend to visit him, on the way to a fun-filled-subject-of-another-book weekend to our house in Montauk, where a very new and improved game of Ring Toss was invented. That made his day. It was certainly a funny crew surrounding my father's bed. It was also very kind of my coworkers to make the visit. They made him laugh and feel like a celebrity himself. On a side note, there's nothing like being stuck on Route 27, the only road out of Montauk, on a summer Sunday, a Holiday no less, in bumper to bumper traffic, with Colin Quinn walking along side everyone's cars interviewing them! Again…subject for another book.

Later that same week, when he came home from the hospital, my mother told me he carried that tape in one hand, his I.V. pole in the other and walked from room to room, popping it in and out of everyone's VCR, showing me off to all who were alive enough to watch.

He was proud.

I'd had many auditions since then. Each one I wanted more than the previous. But, in this case, for this specific audition I was going on, I felt like I was running out of time. I wanted my father to see me work. I needed him to see the fruits of his encouragement, support and love. I needed him to see me do the work he had always wanted to do.

I had a screen test for *One Life To Live*. I didn't get the role. I've even forgotten what the role was, but I'll never forget the casting director. I called after I was told I didn't get the part and asked to speak with her. I am sure she thought I was calling to find out why I hadn't been hired. But because she was the compassionate woman she was and still is, she was not surprised by my explanation. I told her I wanted my father to see me do something other than dance in Lycra before he died. She gave me a copy of my screen test on the down low. My father and I watched it together. His eyes shone. When it was over, he thanked me. He also mimed why he thought I didn't get the role by pointing at my boobs and indicating FLAT and pointing at the girl who got the role (I had her screen test on the tape as well) indicating HUGE! For days he watched that tape over and over again. In a very small way, I guess I had accomplished what I had set out to do: give my father the chance to vicariously live his dream and make fun of my little boobs.

I was thinking about all of these moments as I waited to be called into the room to read. I also thought about them as I left the building to head east. Only this time I was crying.

I had ruined the audition.

Everything about my reading was awful.

I think I thought that I could somehow save my father if I had gotten a job; that because his forty-eighth birthday was the next day, we were all owed some great present. I sobbed the whole train ride home. I couldn't face my father and hoped that he had forgotten where I had been. In case he did ask, I was prepared to throw him off with the pretzel I always brought him from the city. Which by this point was a cold, hard, brick of a thing slathered with mustard.

Just the way I felt. Sans mustard.

*****

Today was my father's birthday. October 30th 1990. I was concerned. How does one wish a dying man a happy birthday?

We had bought cards. One was from Matthew and me and one from my mother. We also bought a cake. My father's favorite, Carvel ice cream cake with those little black, crunchy things.

We sang.

"Happy Birthday to you! Happy Birthday to you! Happy Birthday, dear Daddy, Happy Birthday to you."

There we were, the three of us standing at his bedside looking down at him looking up at us not knowing whom we were and why we were making so much fucking noise.

He didn't know it was his birthday.

The celebration was for us. We didn't know if he would remember. But to save ourselves the guilt of overlooking this day, we selfishly pointed it out to him.

We were doubly damned.

We tenuously balanced between calling his attention to us, to life, to his birthday and ignoring such occasions and allow him to travel his path to the unknown away from us. The social worker assigned to us explained the various stages of dying. The "dying process" it is called. Its stages range from coldness in the digits and appendages to the dark color of the patients urine, to what is horrifically called and even more horrifically sounding "death rattle" or "Cheyne-Stokes" breathing, to finally, sleep.

It is a morbid twelve-step program without the coins.

Today, we dealt with sleep. My father is at peace when

he sleeps. It is we have learned, his detachment process. As he nears death, his world among the living becomes smaller and smaller until all we are is an ebbing echo and all that is ahead of him is light and people he once knew who live in the light. They call to him in warmth and safety. In their world in the light, there is no pain, no injections, no morphine drips, no chemotherapy, no radiation, no pills, no doctors, and no fear. There is only peace.

By calling him back to us, to remembering his birthday, we force him, selfishly, to reconnect with a world he knows he is leaving. With that reintroduction, we force him to muse on his life, the stories, the people, his loves and ultimately the terrifying acknowledgment that every time he closes his eyes may be the last time he sees us.

His birthday is a celebratory occasion for me, blessed to be of him.

But it blessedly means nothing to he who awaits his death.

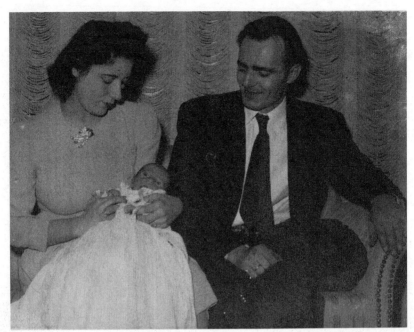

Dad's Christening 1942 (by the way all my daughters were Christened in that gown)

Dad playing football...he's not fuzzy just the picture

An early picture of my Dad

SIZE 40R
HEIGHT 5'11"
WEIGHT 160
WAIST 32
INSEAM 31
SHIRT 15½-34
HAIR Black
EYES Brown
SHOE 10D
HAT 7
GLOVE 9
NOSE 15
COMMERCIAL—TV
(ALL SPORTS)

MATT
COPPOLA

One of my Dad's earlier modeling cards

SEP · 65

Mom and Dad on a date in 1965

Dad and his surfboard in Montauk

One of the first pictures of Dad and me...could I have
adored him anymore?

Matthew and me feeding the ducks

Matthew and me in 1978

Our Christmas tree in the early 1980's

Matthew and Dad right after Dad's surgery 1980

Matthew, Dad and me right after Dad's surgery 1980

Christmas in 1980 after Dad's surgery

Mom, Dad, and me after Dad's surgery in 1981

My Mom

My Mom and me

Mom and me in 1993 at an *Another World* holiday party

All of us at my Confirmation...I think

My parents with my Dad's parents

Mom, Dad, and me 1987

Gils and me in Martha's Vineyard 1984

Colin Quinn and me on the set of *Remote Control* in 1989

My July 20, 1993 *Soap Opera Digest* article

STAR

There's No Heart Coppola's Sleeve; On Alicia It's All Inside

By Stephanie Sloane

(Lorna Devon, ANOTHER WORLD)

In my mind, we've all had difficult things happen to us. Get over it, deal with it and move on." Tough words from a young 20-something woman — but ANOTHER WORLD's Alicia Coppola hasn't let the hand that life dealt her bring her down.

Although Coppola describes her childhood as "idyllic," at the tender age of 12, she was forced to grow up — fast. Her father was diagnosed with brain cancer, and the little girl had to deal with some very adult realities. "When my father was first diagnosed, everything kind of changed," she explains. "All of a sudden, that little niche that was created for us was threatened. I remember my brother, Matthew, didn't smile for years. All of a sudden, we understood the fragility of life, so from that moment on, we were no longer children, really. We realized we couldn't take advantage of anything or anyone at any time.

"In some ways, we became tighter because we were fighting for something," she continues. "But in other ways, we were falling apart. It was like we were on

Birthday: April 12•**Height:** 5'8"or 5'9" • **Hails From:** Huntington, NY• **Words To Live By:** "Life is just too short to sit around and wallow and make yourself miserable. It isn't going to get you anywhere."• **College Major:** "The concentration was basically philosophy. I studied the classics for my first two years and then studied Hitler and the czars of Russia to basically find out why man needs a leader."• **Her Brother's Fear:** "Matthew said, 'You have to promise me you'll never do *Playboy*. At least not while I'm in college, and not when I have any friends — I'll be hazed to death!"

E.J. CARR

67

99

Linda Dano and me July 2012

Mila, Esmé, Greta and me

Anthony and me

My *Star Trek Voyager* trading card

My *NCIS* trading card

Skeet Ulrich, Brad Beyer and me on the set of *Jericho*

Skeet Ulrich and me on the set of *Jericho*

Chapter Eight

"My soul is crushed. My spirit sore;
I do not like me anymore."

Symptom Recital
Dorothy Parker[4]

NOVEMBER 1990

It is about 4:30 in the morning. I hear a loud, perfectly timed cadence of footsteps, like an entire platoon is marching through my house. I open my eyes and see, as if I am in every room of the house at once, my father naked and stomping to the beat. Marching in place. LEFT LEFT LEFT RIGHT LEFT. I DON'T KNOW BUT I BEEN TOLD...SOUND OFF LEFT LEFT LEFT RIGHT LEFT...

His eyes are wild and he is grunting with each step, knees brought high to his chest. Stomping. He comes into my room and screams.

"I AM ALIVE. DIDN'T YOU REALIZE THAT? DIDN'T YOU *KNOW?*"

Rats are swarming at his marching feet...

I awake.

Afraid to stay in my own room, I went into the library, my personal oasis, pulled out the Castro Convertible and lay down. I figured maybe if my father, the marching psychopath, didn't find me in my room to torment me, he would look no further.

That's how real this dream was.

I must have slept for about two or three hours when my mother found me and woke me up.

"Your father's in a coma and Missy, your cat, is dead. Matthew is waiting for you outside with a shovel. Go bury her in the yard."

With that, she, her cigarette and glass of scotch at 8:00 in the fucking morning, excused herself.

"Good morning to you too." I murmured.

She was right. Missy, my cat of twelve years was indeed dead. She was lying outside like an over-loved, balding, stuffed animal a child had finally outgrown and discarded.

Matthew had begun digging.

"I have the feeling this isn't the only grave we'll be digging." He said.

No shit.

We buried Missy in the backyard. Then we went back into the house to deal with our father in the coma.

It wasn't a *true* coma. He was just sleeping really deeply, big-old faker. Probably just wanted to get out of burying the cat, for Christ sakes. Because when he awoke he decided he wanted Ravioli.

Ravi-fucking-oli!

The man had not a bite to eat since the birthday cake we forced on him about a week ago.

The social worker said this too, was normal.

Part of the detachment process. Dying process.

Apparently there's a lot of processing to be done when you are dying. I imagine it's akin to standing on line to complete the paperwork to get a Drivers License at the DMV.

FOR ETERNITY.

Food is too temporal. He still takes water but food is too difficult for his body to deal with. There really isn't any need for it any longer.

But he asked for ravioli, so we gave him ravioli. He ate the whole thing. This act of eating, of literally cleaning his plate once again spun us uncontrollably into an eddy of self-doubt and confusion. If he is lucid enough to ask for ravioli, we wonder if we have done right by him. We've stopped the treatments, stopped the drugs. We have kept him home with us, instead of the hospital. We have done our best to make him

106

comfortable.

But? Yet? However. Hmmmmm. What if? Was it enough? Was it right? When he eats after days of starvation, we wonder if he is getting better. Have we been starving him unknowingly? Has he wanted to eat all these days but could not find the words to tell us? Since we equate food with comfort, with caring and love, we question.

Have we been neglecting him, relegating him to his room to be alone to starve and wither and cry and die, alone? When he cries from his room when he is alone, does he hate us for trying to let him go? Does he feel deserted? Abused? Abandoned?

When he looks upward from his bed with his hand extended toward God, is he asking, pleading to go? Is there someone, something only he can see hovering above him caressing his hand preparing him for his final journey?

When he lowers his arm and tears spill from his eyes we realize that he realizes it's simply not yet time and that he must continue to live in pain.

But when we are quiet, my father and I, when I sit with him in his room and watch him breathe, I see him.

I see his soul soaring fast and furious towards Jesus; trying with all his might to bust through, break through this living barrier to freedom. When his arm drops from reaching, his eyes close and his head turns from me, I know he does not sleep. He musters his strength to lift his arm higher and reach farther and further in attempt to make his final escape.

I am left with pain I cannot heal, fear I cannot quell and confusion I cannot quiet.

I am, I think, going insane.

*****

I go out with George. Or maybe it was Jim, my neighbor. They blend. No, it was Jim, the older brother of one of Matthew's girlfriends. I don't remember where he took me.

To dinner, drinks, a movie, it was all the same. I smoked and stared straight ahead out the windshield as he drove me home. It was snowing, beautiful white raining down hard, pelting the glass of the windshield with its soft iciness. The white was taking over the blackness of the night and of the pavement we were rolling over. Cigarettes taste good in icy air. An ashy staleness mixed with cool frost, a God given menthol. They are especially handy at keeping nonsmokers at a distance.

Not Jim, though.

I knew he was going to park outside my house. I knew he was going to do this under the guise of keeping his one-sided conversation going when really all he wanted was to kiss me.

Fine whatever. I inhaled, exhaled, flicked the stubby butt out the window and let him make his move.

Like I cared.

Like a somnambulist, I sat through his purring and petting and groping and waited for him to be done. I didn't want to go inside. I never knew as Dorothy Parker stated, "what fresh hell" awaited me in there. I just wanted out of this car, out from under this man's hands. I said goodnight, lit up and left him.

I found my mother in the den. Sitting in front of a roaring fire holding a cigarette and a glass of wine. It might have been a romantic setting; a freshly bathed, pretty woman waiting alluringly for her man by a cozy fire, by sliding glass doors that showed the magnificent white snow falling outside. It could have been that but only if you didn't know that by then the pretty woman had probably downed a few Xanax after feverishly reviewing her man's morphine chart to make sure she hadn't overdosed him.

"How was your night? Do you like Jim?" She asked.

I laughed. She laughed. We stayed like that, laughing together for a while. It was nice, an impromptu party in honor of the ridiculousness of her questions.

The next night, Matthew was sitting in the den watching

television. He heard loud, floor shaking footsteps in the hall by the sliding pocket door to the den. He looked up and saw Dad naked, hopping on both feet towards him. His arms were folded over his chest and his right leg was pumping up and down. His eyes were crazed and fixed on Matthew. Towards him he hopped and when he was about five feet away, he fell over like a tree and died.

Another strange dream.

We asked the Social Worker what these dreams that we were having meant. She said that there are reasons why we dream or even daydream these frightening images. We so long to remember our father as vital, agile, healthy and free, that we overemphasize these qualities to the point of perversion.

Matthew, in pure Gotti style, no longer sits with his back to any door in our house. I no longer sleep in my bedroom. We are both afraid of loud footsteps.

The Social Worker says these reactions are normal. My mother records Dad's morphine injections into a chart she has designed for just this purpose. He's been ill for ten years yet she has never done this. She has always known which meds were to be taken at which time by rote. Now she has to record it all, so that on paper, she'll know she didn't kill him. She fantasizes and then obsesses that she's given him too much, too soon and will stare at him for signs, like she'd know them anyway, of an overdose. Her mind plays tricks on her and even though somewhere deeply embedded in our minds, where a few threads of sanity may still exist, we know we haven't OD'd our father and that he does not hop and march and yell and rant.

We no longer trust ourselves.

*****

I went into the city to see Ned. Instead of staying at his place uptown, he was at his mother's in the Village. He took me to some little out of the way restaurant and asked me a question I had no idea how to answer.

"Do you have any love for me?" He asked, quietly and with a sincerity that struck me dumb.

"Do I have any love for you?" I, in equal sincerity, repeated back.

"Yes." He said.

"Of course not. I have no love for you. I have no love for anyoneanythinganywheREATANYTIME. I AM WITHOUT LOVE AND HOW DARE YOU ASK ME THAT NOW!"

"I just wanted to know where I stand with you."

"You stand nowhere."

Why we went back to his parents' place, I don't know. Perhaps it was too late for me to take a train. In any event, he poured me a drink and tried to apologize which just made me angrier and I threw my drink and the glass at the wall and went downstairs to sleep.

I don't know what he did, but in the morning he wasn't there and I was alone in a strange apartment and for a second it felt like I had a different life or was on vacation and that felt nice.

But Ned kept calling me on his parents' phone. I could hear him talking on the answering machine. He was sorry.

Sorry for making me think of love and relationships and boyfriends and girlfriends and the stuff of the living when I was enmeshed in the stuff of the dead. I knew he meant well. I knew he was merely protecting himself, as he most assuredly should. I hope to hell he erased those messages before his parents came home. Had they heard them, I doubt they ever would have dared go out of town again.

I had a lot of male attention during this time. George, Jim, Ned... The pathology of this is not fucking lost on me. I am not an idiot. I knew that because I could not get attention from the one person from whom I craved it, I sought it elsewhere. I just couldn't give it back. Not in the way they wanted.

Damn Ned for asking. Damn him for making me feel like the shallow, empty shell I had become. I wanted to feel. So I allowed myself to crumble in the arms of these men and let them take my anger. Let them take only bits of me while I took much of them, filling me with enough of their vitality to last until I had used it up. Then I went back for more. Didn't matter really from whom. They all offered me the same thing, disguised in different packaging, adoration, love, physical contact, whatever. They were filling stations. Pure and simple.

My need to be full, full of anything was insatiable.

Because really, truth be told, the only thing I was full of was shit.

What confused me, what really confounded the hell out of me, was their constant presence. My aloofness, my apathy towards them only made them want to be around me more. It's not like I was sleeping with any of them, because I wasn't. It wasn't like I was a lot of fun to be around, because I wasn't. It wasn't like I offered stimulating conversation, because half the time I wasn't even listening to them in the first place. It wasn't like they were looking to take advantage of an incredibly fucked up and vulnerable girl, because while I may have both fucked up and vulnerable, I was neither weak nor stupid.

I reasoned that my misanthropic melancholy was lighting the way of the moths.

I was wrong.

Turns out they were just nice guys who wanted me to love them.

THANKSGIVING 1990

What can I say? We went through the motions. We cooked and prayed and ate. I recalled the Thanksgiving from ten years ago at my uncle's house and all I could think of was the song "You're So Far Away," by Carole King. It was playing on the radio in the car as we drove away from the hospital to share Thanksgiving dinner with my uncle's family, who wasn't MY family. Though I am a huge Carole King fan, I fucking hate that song.

After helping my mother clean up, I went out with Brad. We went to the junior high school baseball field. We went to third on second. This is the first and only time I will ever mention Brad.

I have hit a new low, even for me. I know why I do what I do. I know it all, but the knowledge of my actions does not prevent the anger. What is it that they say in Alcoholics Anonymous: "Discover, Discard, Release?" Well, I have discovered and Lord knows I have discarded. But I cannot release. That would mean I have to repent the rage. Without the rage, who am I?

Chapter Nine

"Could you put your light on please, it's kind of dark tonight.
And I feel a little lonely, yes, I need a little light.
Could you put your light on please, let me hear a friendly sound.
I could make it through 'til morning if you could let your light shine down."

"Could You Put Your Light On Please"
Harry Chapin

DECEMBER 1, 1980

My first radiation treatment. Ransohoff said I could receive them at Huntington Hospital as an outpatient. I was to have 5400 rads administered, 100 rads per day. The first two treatments were to be on my left side, and the next one on my right side. That alternating pattern would be followed because my tumor had been just a little left of center. They laid me on a table and pinpointed where the radiation would be administered with an X-ray type graph paper. Then they marked four-inch lines on both sides of my head with an indelible red marker as a guide for the therapist. Then they took a Polaroid of my marked head for their files.

They told me not to wash it off in the weeks to come. I felt like a guinea pig – a laboratory animal. It was humiliating; it was the first time I felt like a slab of meat since the entire ordeal began. I had hoped they would use some kind of invisible ultraviolet sensitive marker. This was a constant reminder of my surgery. Luckily, winter was approaching and I wore my stocking cap most of the time to hide the constant reminder.

The days of the treatments were endless. My dad would pick me up at 8 AM and take me to the hospital for my 8:15 appointment. I was the second one on the table each morning. I experienced no discomfort during the administration of the dose. Unlike many people, I felt no nausea or other side effects. However, during those thirty-one days of treatment, I was deeply depressed. My dad would drive me home and I would go back to sleep. I was tired and foul mooded. They were really the dog days. I didn't look the way I used to, the left side of my head was swollen with fluid, I didn't feel the way I used to and I wasn't the man I used to be. I wondered if I would ever become that man again.

During that time, Linda had her business offices downstairs in our basement. She had six secretaries working downstairs and it seemed they were up and down every ten minutes. One to make coffee, one to check on it. When it was ready they all trooped up to get some. Then it was lunchtime. One made soup, one had lunch in our refrigerator or oven and one chopped up a salad. They all sat around our kitchen table while Linda and I had to sit quietly in our den. Their cars were parked in our driveway like a parking lot. Our whole house was completely taken over until 5, 5:30 PM. We had absolutely no privacy.

Every day the same routine. My dad would pick me up and drive me to the hospital for my treatment. I would return home, sit in the den and fall asleep. There were a couple of weeks there when I wore the same clothes to sleep, not bothering or caring to change. It was just too much of an effort. Linda would prod me to get going, not quite understanding what I was going through and not quite knowing how to handle it. She had pressures, related to her business, since she had fallen so far behind due to my stay in the hospital. My depression was compounding our problems. I would be listless, not wanting to go on and she would try, in vain, to pick me up. It was one of the lowest points in our relationship – yet it would prove to strengthen our marriage and love for one another. If you make it through something like that you can make it through anything.

DECEMBER 20, 1980

We tried to get ourselves "up" for Christmas for the kid's sake as well as our own. We bought a Christmas tree on the Saturday before Christmas and I rearranged some furniture in the living room to make room for it. A big mistake. After decorating 115 the tree that night, I felt a slight twinge of pain around my heart. By Sunday afternoon it had become a full-blown case of very real excruciating pain in my chest and back. It hurt with every breath. I couldn't lie on my front. I couldn't even walk without a shooting pain in my chest. The only comfortable position was sitting forward with two pillows between my lap and chest; it was the only way that allowed me to breathe. We called three or four doctors. Their answering services called back to refer us to other doctors covering for them. None of them could see me until Monday in their offices. Finally, after exhausting all possibilities, Linda called our neighbor, a gynecologist. She seemed to think it was an Intercostal muscle pull, but just in case it wasn't, she suggested I call the emergency room at Huntington Hospital to tell them I was on my way. She would do the same.

I didn't exactly get a brass band reception. When I arrived and explained my problem, that I was on the verge of collapsing because of the pain, a nurse said, "Just sit over there."

I said, "I can't sit."

She replied, "Then stand over there."

After pacing back and forth for half an hour, getting angrier by the minute, I went back to the nurse's station and pleaded, "Please help me or give me something for the pain. Didn't Dr. Murita call?"

"Oh," she said, "You're the One."

At that point I was so angry, in so much pain and so goddamned irritated that I said to Linda, "Let's get the hell out of here. I'll take care of myself." She agreed because she was just as angry.

We made our way back to the car with me taking tiny baby steps, so as not to disturb the area giving me pain. We drove home in silence. When we arrived we realized we had been in such a hurry to get to the hospital that we had left our house keys on the kitchen table. We were locked out. There we were, standing outside the house in freezing, overcast gloom, returning from yet another disappointment. It was the straw that broke the camel's back. It all seemed so hopeless – what was the point of going on like this?

116

Linda broke down and started to cry in anger and frustration, cursing the whole world. Then it was my turn. We just stood there like two lost sheep crying in each other's arms. I guess it was then that we both decided that we couldn't go on like this; that we MUST survive and we MUST pick each other up when we sense that the other is down. We stood there and decided that if we were to survive, we had to help each other. I finally broke a garage window and she managed to get inside and open the door for me. She sat down and laughed till she cried some more. I couldn't. It hurt too much.

DECEMBER 22, 1980

When I went for my radiation treatment on Monday, I told the radiologist, Dr. Elenhoff, about my chest pain and my experience in the emergency room the day before. He took an x-ray of my chest, thinking that perhaps I had cracked a rib or two. There were no cracked ribs, but he did see a dark spot on my lung. He told me it could be a pulmonary embolism. I said, "Don't be ridiculous, don't you think someone would have noticed that before?" The idea was so preposterous that I dismissed it. But he insisted I get a lung scan anyway. Of course there was no pulmonary embolism and when I told Linda about this, she began having her doubts about the radiologist too.

CHRISTMAS 1980

My parents had invited Linda, myself and the children to their home for the traditional seven fish dinner that all Italian families of their generation still observe on Christmas Eve. I told my dad that I would prefer not to come. I wanted to have Christmas Eve in _my_ home with _my_ family. Besides, I really wasn't in any shape to be going anywhere. My father said, "Your mother will be hurt if you don't come." I said, "I'll talk to her."

On the Tuesday before Christmas Eve my mom and I sat down and talked. I explained that I didn't want to hurt her, but I 117 was just not ready to be exposed to the rest of the family. I felt my presence might dampen the festivities. She said, "They're family. They'll understand." I held my ground and repeated to her that I wanted to be with _my_ family, _my_ wife and _my_ children. Then she understood.

At Christmas dinner we clasped hands around the table. Finally we were alone together and could reflect what was happening in our lives. Linda led a simple prayer of thanks for simply allowing us all to be together.

At about 9 PM Lin and I decided to go into the den and relax, biding our time until the kids fell asleep. They were both very excited about what Santa Claus was going to bring them the next morning. We had the presents hidden in the basement. As I was lying on the couch I began to feel tingling in my arms and fingertips. I had felt tingling before, but never this intense. I had no feeling in my arms and hands. Naturally I called the local MD who, naturally, was out and didn't want to be disturbed on Christmas Eve. We then tossed around the idea of calling Ransohoff. We thought the tingling might somehow be related to the surgery. The numbing sensation was getting worse and we both became frightened enough to call him. His service said he was upstate with his family and gave us the phone number. We just missed him as he had gone out with his grandchildren. We left a message to return our call.

Of course after my call the tingling subsided and I began to get the feeling back in my hands. I felt silly calling him in such a panic. I thought maybe I had been lying on a nerve or something. With that thought the phone rang and it was Ransohoff. I explained what had happened. He said, "Don't worry about it. It's got nothing to do with your surgery. You were probably lying in an awkward position. I should be so healthy. Don't worry about it. So you're a jock with a little j. Have a Merry Christmas."

You can imagine how relieved I felt. I was 200% better than before his call. It's amazing how a little thing like Ransohoff returning my call on Christmas Eve can mean so much when you're in such a vulnerable state. It reinforced our trust and belief in Ransohoff as a truly dedicated doctor and a kind and caring individual. He may not have the best bedside manner, but when it really counts, the man comes through.

NEW YEARS EVE 1980

We went to Lynn and Jon's for New Years Eve. It is a tradition that goes back to when we first became friends. We alternate homes each year, staying over with the kids so that everyone is together and no one is on the road. Lynn prepared her usual last minute dinner, which we all enjoyed and laughed about. We waited to ring out the absolute worst year of our lives. Pouring the champagne, we wished for a better 1981. We all realized that we are mortal. Life is very fragile – if you don't have your health, nothing you may have is of much value.

Chapter Ten

"Childhood Toyland
Mystical merry Toyland
Once you pass its borders
You can never return again."

"Toyland"[5]

DECEMBER 1990

Today was a hard one: A good one because I got to spend all day with my father but a hard one because I got to spend all day with my father. Let's see... first thing this morning, I gave him a sponge bath. This takes awhile because I wash, dry and lotion each part of his body at a time, separately. First the right arm, then the left, and on and on until he is squeaky clean and lovingly lotioned. The lotion keeps the bedsores at bay. Then I changed the bed sheets with him still in the bed. Sounds harder than it is really. It's really just the matter of undoing one side of the bed, pushing the sheets right up to my father's body, turning him onto his side, then pulling the sheets out from under him. It's the same thing when putting the sheets on the bed, only in reverse. I think he feels much better resting on clean sheets. Then I put a new hospital gown on him and then the best part... I shaved his face.

This is my favorite thing to do with my father. I propped him up against pillows, handed him a hand mirror and went to work. I use an electric razor. It provides me with more precision and a lot less clean up. Tiny scissors trim the more delicate areas around his lips, nose and ears and then a little make-up brush to whisk away the trimmings. It took me about half and hour and when I was done he looked into the mirror to check my work. He smiled. That told me I had done good.

We have hospice nurses who come every day. They vary.

My relationship to them is strenuous.

I hate them.

They trot in and out of our house like a bad Halloween parade. They're only costumed as nurses. These are not women who love caring for the sick and elderly. No. Most of them are miserable, dowdy, vagrants either looking to steal or take out their miserable lives on those who can't defend themselves. One in particular was rough with my father when she thought I was in the kitchen. Nothing violent, but nothing gentle either. I threw her out so fast both our heads spun.

They were, I guess, more knowledgeable than we on the needs of a dying person, but care for my father they do not. WE do. After all, why shouldn't it be my job at twenty-one years of age to check my father's catheter? Why shouldn't I have that up close and personal of a relationship with my father's penis, after all, I did once reside in it. Why shouldn't I have to be the one checking to see if his urine is darkening in color or is more or less frequent? Why shouldn't I be hearing his cries, cleaning his body and medicating his sores? Why shouldn't I be doing these things? You know why? Because I simply shouldn't be, that's why. It is all simply not what I should be doing. They are supposed to do these things. Sometimes they do them, other times I do. I, in turn, resent this and embrace this.

Sometimes I hate my mother for not protecting me from everything I've seen and done.

But then I remember.

He didn't shirk off the caring for me onto someone else.

He heard my cries.

He cleaned my body.

He kissed my boo-boos.

A perfect circle. He was there when I came into the world. I'll be there when he leaves it.

Tonight we got a baby sitter for my father. That doesn't even sound right. But we did. We needed to get out of the house and the Chapin's were having a Christmas party so we got Dad a sitter. The man, the sitter, was from hospice. It's not a good feeling, leaving my father alone with a stranger. I was not comfortable with it. All sorts of horrible things went through my mind; images of the sitter abusing or neglecting my father, or even worse, my father calling out to us and never getting an answer. But I guess our need to unwind and forget for one night trumped my father's needs.

Like we could unwind and forget anyway. Like one night is going to make a huge fucking difference. Like I really want to be around a group of holiday well-wishers, twinkling lights, reindeer cookies and eggnog swilling, cheerful Christmasy motherfuckers.

So many people were there. So many people wanting to ask how my father was doing. They don't know how. Even though their intentions are good, anything and everything they say is just assaulting. It's not like he has a cold. He's not going to get better, so they can't say, "Hope he gets better soon!" No. He's dying. What can people say? Hope he dies well? Soon?

That's it.

Hope he dies better soon.

Come on.

We drank, tried to chat, be cheerful, drank some more.

Came home.

Should never have left home in the first place.

*****

People have been dropping by. "Paying their respects", as we Italian Americans call it. We also like to say things "fell off the truck," about whatever new television or stereo or set of pots and pans we might have. At my cousin's house, almost everything they have "fell off the truck." When I was a kid I used to imagine random trucks driving by with their hatch wide open as everything just spilled out onto the road, everyone grabbing whatever the loot was. To this day if anyone asks me where I got a dress or a pair of shoes… "They fell off the truck!"

That's why I love UPS; things just fall off the truck.

Anyway, Uncle Paulie-with-the-piece came by. He sat down in the chair next to my father's side of the bed revealing a black, shiny Glock strapped to his ankle. Yet another thing Italian Americans do apparently. Interesting seeing a large, heavyset man strapping heat, crying like a baby as he walked out of the room.

Coach Crawley also stopped by. He's the stepfather of one of Matthew's friends from school and a friend of my father's from I don't know where. I was lying beside my father when Coach walked into the room.

"Breaks my heart." He said.

I left them alone to visit. Another 6 ft. something guy leaves in tears.

These two men are etched in my memory because they came. They took time out of their lives to say hello to my father, not goodbye. It didn't seem like goodbye the way they did it. They laughed with Dad. They held him. They talked about whatever grown men talk about. Well, maybe Uncle Paulie-with-the-piece talked about different things. But I don't judge. What I would have given to be a fly on that wall. The point is I remember them for their kindness.

Our neighbors? They're a horse of different color all together. These men, my father's supposed friends, they who barbequed with my dad borrowed his tools and drank his beer, never, not once came by. Except for one. Gary. He loved my dad. He lived around the corner. Divorced with two little boys and as I recall drunk most of the time. When my father was in Philadelphia in the hospital, Gary drove through the night to visit him. A nice gesture, we all thought, until we all realized he was drunk. Another time he came to visit Dad and again drunk, called me a cunt for not letting him in. This is the same man who years before in 1978, the winter of the blackout, came into my room during dinner (our house was the only one with a gas oven and stove range instead of electric, so we cooked for the entire street) and tried to lie down with me on my bed.

Drunk.

He did not succeed but I am sure this incident alone might explain a bit of the anxiety that I have portrayed on these very pages. Whatever. No one got hurt.

At least his heart, when it came to my father, was in the right place. The rest of them? Cowards. Every last fucking one of them.

Not one family on our street, the street we'd lived on for almost fifteen years, asked to see my father, asked how we were, asked how he was. My father became the white elephant in the room everyone saw but didn't talk about.

Nice holiday warmth.

Today I had to tell Grandma we wouldn't be spending Christmas Eve or Christmas day with them this year.

Why this was my job, I'll never know. But I know this. My Grandmother is one frightening little Italian Matriarch. The Godfather has nothing on her. Don Corleone? A pussy.

She scared the shit out of me. She started crying and grasping at my sweater sleeve like a toddler trying to keep mommy from leaving. It was awful. She kept wailing over and over "HE'S MY SON! MY SON! THE FAMILY NEEDS TO BE TOGETHER!" She would not let me leave. She would not let me go. She would not stop. She simply would not STOP! I didn't know what to do. Then I knew why I was given this job. My mother couldn't handle it. Just like everything else. If something were too hard, get the kids to do it.

"We're in this together." She says.

"We stick together." She says.

Until something ugly needs doing and then it's "tell your grandmother we aren't going to see them for Christmas. If it

125

comes from you, she'll understand."

Bullshit.

If it comes from me, my mother won't have to deal with it.

My mother did have a point. My grandparents agitate my father. They don't mean to. But their pacing and crying in front of him has to stop. No one wants to see that for Christmas, so it's better this way. Besides, Matthew and I want our father to ourselves. What's left of him and what's left of us.

*****

George left us today. He's taking some Deejay job in Europe of all places. He'll leave after the New Year. He wrote me a poem and drew a picture for me for Christmas. I gave him a gold cross necklace that my father had indicated he wanted George to have. It was sad. My dad knew he couldn't keep George here with us, we all knew that. Much as we wanted to be selfish and keep this lovely man to ourselves to care for Dad as beautifully and gracefully as he did, we wanted George to go and find his own bit of peace. I went to see PURPLE RAIN alone and cried through it. It was the worst most beautiful movie I have ever seen. I understood George's fascination with Prince at that moment. Prince was just a boy looking to be accepted and loved. Cliché and true, open and simple and naive. Just like George.

Some point later, could have been days or weeks, I went to George's house to see his brother, my old friend and ended up speaking to his mother in her over decorated kitchen. She inferred in her cruel words that she worried that her eldest son would never amount to anything. I inferred to her in my own cruel words that if she could only take off her chintz colored glasses for just a second she would see that her eldest son was the only son for whom she should *never* worry because he was the only one in their family whose "anything," in our book, amounted to a whole fucking lot.

126

It's amazing how a little cancer makes things a whole lot clearer.

*****

We got a tree.

Mom, Matthew and I decorated it. Our Christmas trees are our family albums so to speak. They have, for 22 years, told the tales of our achievements, interests, loves and desires. Our mother made sure of that. Each year she would give Matt and I ornaments that represented our endeavors for that year. It's a really wonderful tradition. Each beautiful ornament, hanging carefully on its branch tells a story of our life.

I can look back and see what my life was about in 3rd grade, 8th grade, senior year of high school and college. We have our own contributions: Popsicle stick designs courtesy of K-2nd grades. We have Mom's ornamental interpretations: porcelain dolls, soccer balls and players, tiny ballet slippers, drummer boys, little flutes and pianos, skiers, masks of comedy and tragedy, little Snoopys, little monkeys, (mine and Matt's nicknames) miniature baseballs, bowling balls, jazz shoes, little lipsticks and a bevy of others. Sometimes we got just one a year. But mostly, mom got us two. That's four a year. That's close to 84 ornaments. My favorite ornament is the very first one my mother gave me. It's a papier-mâché doll. She looks like a fairy or Mr. Heat Miser. She has an orange dress and flaming orange hair. She has stick legs and little elfin shoes with curled up toes. Her head is falling off. I think my father tried to stick a toothpick through her head to keep it on, because she now has a stick for a neck.

If you turn her over, on her butt, you'll see the words "Alicia 1968." On each of these ornaments our names and the year are written.

Our stories are recorded on the asses of dolls.

This year we added syringes and bottles of morphine.

We brought Dad out in his wheelchair and sat him in front of the tree. His face lit up. He regarded it like it was the 127 most splendid tree he has ever seen. He stared so hard and so long at it, like he was absorbing every last detail to take with him: the flickering white lights, the brightly colored balls, the glitter of tinsel hung delicately strand by strand like Mom taught us, the star brilliant atop the highest branch and most important, each ornament, signifying every step his children took.

The beauty of a Christmas tree is always, to me, overwhelming. It is without a doubt the thing I look forward to all year. For my father who was seeing it for the last time, it was truly a gift. He took pictures with his heart. I know when he is going to wherever it is he is going, he will take these pictures of his family standing before a tree decorated with stories and childhood art and he will feel, no, he will *know*, that his was a full and complete life.

He looked and saw and had a seizure.

He fell back in his wheelchair, his head missing by an inch the bricks of the fireplace step and passed right out. It took the three of us to carry him back to his room.

And,

Scene.

*****

CHRISTMAS EVE 1990

Who cares?

CHRISTMAS DAY 1990

No one.

NEW YEARS EVE 1990

Amateur night. The eve of a New Year gives assholes the

license to misbehave, drink way too much and drive.

I went to a party with my friend David. I figured it would do me good to get out of the house (as I have stated before, ANY reason to get out of the house was welcomed) and have a bit of fun. Matthew was headed out with his girlfriend Jaime and Mom was staying home with Dad, grateful for the time alone with him.

Everyone I grew up with was there; the "best friend" and her entourage and the stoner kids who are now stoner adults. George's was a welcoming face to see. Obviously, he hadn't left yet and we were able to catch up. As always he was kind and soft spoken and had only words of love for my family. It was a shining moment in an otherwise very dark night.

David drank too much. Everyone did. He was my ride, so I called a cab. My mother's words came back to me: "Always bring enough cash for a phone call and a cab." Sage advice.

I returned home to find my mother, Matthew and Jaime sitting in the den. My mother was comforting and consoling Jaime as she continually vomited into my mother's prized lobster pot as Matthew looked on in horror and compassion. Apparently she, too, had been given the license to misbehave and drink way too much. At least Matthew drove.

My mother had enough. Pride overwhelmed her because her children were home before the stroke of the New Year, sober and safe, but anger overcame her as well because I think she thought we should have been given the license too, to cut loose and be kids and have fun. We should have been the partiers, the one's throwing up in the lobster pot. I think she felt we were cheated out of our New Years celebration because our feelings of responsibility towards her and our father won out over that fun.

I think tonight was the night she finally realized that Matthew and I had grown up way too fast.

NEW YEARS DAY 1991

Matthew came home with a surprise for Dad. A tattoo 129

of the word MUNK now adorned his upper left thigh. Munk is our father's nickname for Matthew; it is short for MONKEY BOY. When Matthew was little, he was a very sickly child. He had a perpetually runny nose, flushed cheeks and terrible ear problems that only got better when the doctor finally put tubes in his ears. Because he never felt well, he was a particularly cuddly boy. He always wanted to be held and snuggled. Once in position he would wrap his arms and legs around mom or dad's body and cling like a little monkey. Thus the moniker.

My nickname was SNOOP. Apparently when I was born, Dad thought I struck a remarkable resemblance to Snoopy, Charlie Brown's faithful canine companion. Why, I don't know. I asked him once and he said it was because I was black and white all over. Sounds like the beginning of a child's riddle "Hey, what's small, white and black all over and screams like a banshee?" Me, I guess. The name stuck and has gone through many a permutation. One of them was SNOOPADOODLE.

Don't even ask.

I was supposed to go with Matthew to get SNOOPADOODLE tattooed across my ass, but I figured, hoped rather, that my father would understand my hesitancy. When Matthew dropped trou and played show and tell, the look on Dad's face was priceless. Even when he's dying, the guy's got gleam -- his eyes had the makings of the devil's play in them.

He liked it! Hell, he loved it! He punched Matthew on the leg with his good arm and said, "Fuck, yeah."

What more could a son ask for?

Chapter Eleven

"Henry: Pierce, are you scared?
Hawkeye: Don't be silly. I'm too frightened to be scared."

MASH
The Army-Navy Game[6]

JANUARY 5, 1981

I still had five more radiation treatments left. On Monday, the day before my last treatment, I asked Dr. Elenhoff what the future procedure would be, thinking that I might have to come back in a month or so for a checkup.

"On Wednesday, you start chemotherapy." He said.

I couldn't believe it. My face registered shock.

"Chemotherapy," he repeated, "to make sure we got it all."

I told him I thought the radiation was supposed to take care of the rest.

"Normally it does," he replied, "but after radiation we normally do chemotherapy as a follow up."

"Oh," pausing long enough to get my thoughts together, "Didn't Ransohoff tell you the chemo was unnecessary?"

"Yes, but we do it here anyway."

I pointed out that he intended to give me chemo without Ransohoff's knowledge and in direct conflict with his instructions.

"Well, I wouldn't exactly put it that way."

"Well then, how exactly would you put it?" I had him. He simply turned around and walked away.

When I got home and told Linda about what he had said, she was furious. Her dad had leukemia a few years before and managed to survive it, but not before suffering through three tortuous years of chemotherapy that almost destroyed the whole family. She refused to accept Dr. Elenhoff's decision. "If Ransohoff says you don't need it then it's Ransohoff's decision! Elenhoff's not going to put us through the agony my father went through! Call Ransohoff immediately!"

I called him and told him what Dr. Elenhoff had in mind. He said, "He's overzealous. I'll call him and set him straight."

JANUARY 6, 1981

I put on a suit and tie to celebrate my last day of treatment. Our minds will conjure an insignificant act and transform a minute personal event into one of very special meaning. Prior to that I had been wearing the same old clothes every day.

My dad picked me up and was surprised to see me dressed up. Or was he? When we arrived at the hospital I was naturally anxious to elicit the conversation between the two "Hoff's," for I <u>knew</u> this was to be my last day of treatment. I saw Elenhoff down the hallway. I called to him. I knew he heard me but kept on going. I became elated. I knew right then that I would not get chemotherapy.

After the last treatment I waited for Dr. Elenhoff to return. I had all day. When he finally did return he said that Ransohoff had called him yesterday. I didn't need the chemo, but he thought I should have it.

I said, "Why do you want to put me through that agony?"

"That's the way we do it here." He said.

"Well, you're not going to use me as a guinea pig for your medical files!" I was really pissed by that time and we both knew it. It was a battle of wills. I refused to play the role of the ignorant patient who doesn't question the doctor.

He handed me Ransohoff's report dated December 2nd, 1980, two days after I was released from the hospital and there was no mention of chemotherapy. I just turned and walked out.

That night Linda and I went out to celebrate our freedom. I felt like it was a milestone. I was anxious to get on with my life, to put things back in order.

For the rest of the month I went to the office late and   133 left early. I know I was there, but I don't remember contributing very much. I was frustrated and confused. My mind was just not functioning properly. I went through the motions but seemed never really to accomplish very much. It all seemed so hopeless. I'd come home at three and go right to sleep. Wake at six, six thirty when Linda got home, eat dinner with her and the children, watch some TV and be back in bed, asleep, by nine. This routine lasted the rest of January and halfway through February.

Along with this dull drab existence, which matched the climate to a tee, was a feeling that I knew best how to take care of myself. Little did I know that every time I skipped taking my pills, I was increasing the possibility of having another seizure and decreasing the healing of my brain. In fact, it precipitated a seizure early one February morning. It not only frightened Linda half to death, but also heightened our fear, anxiety and frustration. I felt as though I would never get well again and was going to have to live with the threat of seizures for the rest of my life. That's no kind of life at all.

We called Dr. Reiser and he told us to meet him at the emergency room at the hospital. He took my blood levels of Dilantin and Phenobarbital. He asked what our prescription read. He seemed to think it was okay for he knew what the dosages meant.

(In November when I checked out of the hospital, you recall, there was no one "official" to say, "Here's your prescription, this is how you take it, etc. You are free to go now." My prescription read 200mgs Dilantin twice a day and 30mgs Phenobarbital three times a day. I asked the male nurse what that meant. He said, "Take one Dilantin twice a day and one pheno three times a day." I assumed that one Dilantin capsule was 200 mgs from what he told me.)

As it turned out, I was on the wrong prescription for almost two and a half months before I had my first postoperative seizure. All that time I should have been taking <u>four</u> Dilantins instead of two. That – and the times I never bothered to take them at all – led to my seizure. I just didn't have enough medication in my system, nor did I know any better. I blame that nurse and myself for my not confirming his interpretation of the dosages with a doctor. Wouldn't you think a licensed nurse would at least be able to read a prescription? That's what I got for not questioning further. Take <u>nothing</u> for granted! Ask until you understand! If you are not <u>completely</u> and I mean <u>completely</u> satisfied with an answer or explanation, find someone who <u>can</u> satisfy you.

PEACE AT LAST 1981

In March we were committed to go to Florida for a week. It was partly business, since Linda's business has an office there, but mostly relaxation. I swam laps in the pool and was surprised that I could do so many. I felt so good that I even swam laps beyond the breakers in the ocean. Linda was very happy with that, but never once took her eyes off me. We celebrated that night at the Breakers Hotel in Palm Beach, the night before we were scheduled to check out.

The next morning I had another seizure and didn't know why. We were so exasperated, frazzled and terrified by this time, we were almost insane with fear. I was taken to a hospital in Palm Beach at 5 AM. Linda called Ransohoff, waking him from a sound sleep, with news of my latest seizure. He said, "I told you brain surgery takes a long time to heal. There are no guarantees."

At that point she was so angry and so frustrated that an unnatural calm came over her. She was ready to accept anything that might happen to me, even my death. She was at the lowest emotional point that I have ever seen her and so was I.

When they found that my medication levels were nonexistent, zero, they gave me massive dosages to get me up to therapeutic level. I had absolutely no Phenobarbital or Dilantin in my system. That's what was causing the seizures. My medication just wasn't enough. I was taking less than before the operation because, once again, I naively trusted a doctor. It was wrong. I needed more, not less. I learned that any intrusion into the brain could in itself cause a seizure. They had gone into my brain and removed a tumor, leaving scar tissue as residue. This alone can 135 cause a seizure, at any time.

From the hospital I went to my father-in-law's house in Delray. I needed sleep after being medicated so heavily. During the day and a half that I spent there a sculptor my father-in-law had commissioned visited the house to discuss his work. When he learned that I had had brain surgery and was recovering from my third seizure he revealed that he was a retired neurosurgeon and was very familiar with Ransohoff's work. He was the one who finally told Linda I had been taking my prescription all wrong, that I should have been taking 400 mgs of Dilantin and 90 mgs of pheno daily: four pills of 100 mgs and three pills of 30 mgs each. He reinforced in my wife and in-laws the fact that I needed correct therapeutic levels of medication for my brain to heal properly. It's like any other wound and needs plenty of time to get back to normal.

He said I'd be all right in a few months, but neither of us should get frustrated or angry, especially me. I was always feeling frustrated because I was so confused about things. My body was fine but my mind was still a bit fuzzy. I couldn't remember little things like where I put my glasses or car keys or my wallet. But this was normal for someone in my condition. We were not to worry about it. Just take one day at a time. Give myself plenty of time to heal.

That's exactly what we needed to hear. It renewed our confidence and resolve. We flew back home with a new lease on life; finally knowing that what was happening to us was normal. Eventually I would get better.

Did Ransohoff tell me about this but I was so involved in getting better and getting on with my life that I didn't listen? Did I think that because I was so healthy before the surgery that I didn't need this medication? After all, I had seldom taken anything stronger than an aspirin. Or, did Ransohoff leave instructions for his staff to tell me which weren't carried out.

It was about this time that the thought of writing this story came to me. I channeled and transformed my frustration into a positive outlet. The more I wrote the less frustrated I became.

*****

1982

It's now almost a year and a half after surgery and things are just about back to normal. My hair is almost grown back. I still have a little fluid around my left temple. I did, however, purchase a wig, which I wear when I am modeling. In fact, I've done more modeling since the operation than before!

The business is still there and running well. As time passed by, I took on more and more responsibilities until I was back to the same old routine; on the phone helping a customer, three incoming calls waiting, two people waiting to see me and a desk piled so high with paperwork that I seemed to peer out from under. Now when I tell people about my surgery they say, "Come on, <u>you</u> had brain surgery?" I have to show them my scar to prove it! So you see – the brain does heal – it just takes time. Furthermore, I play tennis better than I used to, I swim <u>more</u> laps every morning and evening and I feel better than I ever have. Once again, I am a Jock with a big J!

Linda's business is thriving. She just opened another branch in Floral Park and moved her corporate offices to larger quarters. She has the normal fears and anxieties about her business as I have about mine. On the surface we appear to be a normal carefree and happy family once again. But there is still an undercurrent. As someone once said, "Once you have known fear, it sits on your shoulder. It never disappears." The crucial fact is that we support each other. If she comes home after a bad day, I'll pick her up, and she does the same for me. If we both come home after a bad day we laugh about it. We still face the same daily problems. Perhaps now, we just see them a little differently. Life goes on. And, we always have the house in Montauk as a haven of peace and solitude.

Chapter Twelve

"Slow curtain.
 The end."

All About Eve
Joseph L Mankiewicz[7]

JANUARY 3, 1991

I was watching television in the den this morning. TV has become a huge part of my life here. When I'm not with my father or sleeping, I'm in front of the TV zoning out, allowing all the useless images passage to my noisy, ugly mind. They help to drown out whatever horrific thing I have just seen, heard or felt in my father's dying room.

I heard a scream. The shrill of a siren. I'll never forget this sound; it is my father crying. I hurdle the couch, the chair, the piano bench and run into his room.

Somehow my father has thrown off his bedclothes. He was holding his head and frantically rubbing his face and beard. He was agitated, very agitated. Agitation, steps seven and eight in the dying process handbook. His breathing was abnormal, panting followed by seconds of no breathing at all. Normal they say. People hold their breath, attempting to suffocate themselves. My father did this a lot. He tries with all his might to hold his breath just that one final second more but his human instinct to survive always steps in and botches his suicide attempt. He always looks depressed afterwards. Disappointed at the lack of control he has over his own body, that it simply won't do what he wants it to do. Normal? To whom?

"She's here." He whispers.

"Who's here?" I ask.

He points upward, towards the ceiling he has become so unfortunately aquatinted with.

"The blue lady with the blue hair." He answers.

"Does she see you?" I ask.

"Yes."

Okay. "What does she want?" I ask both afraid and hopeful of the answer…

"Me."

He closes his eyes, lowers his arm and begins to once again rub his face and head as if soothing from the outside the pressure of the tumor within. He cries louder, his siren alarming the people who are not yet coming for him. The longer he waits the louder he cries.

I am afraid.

"Can I hold your hand, Daddy?" I ask him.

He lowers his eyes. He no longer sees me. He grasps my hand. Together, hands clasped palm like in prayer, we will the blue lady with the blue hair to come.

*****

We just got back inside the house. It's 3:30 in the morning. We couldn't sleep so we went outside. It has been snowing. A beautiful white enveloping our street with the muffled crunch of snowflakes hitting drifted snow. The moon shone light that glittered on the whiteness like a million fallen stars. It is cold and icy and peaceful and glistening. Matthew and I walked gingerly, not wanting to mar the perfect landscape with our footprints and at intervals flung ourselves backwards into the snow, moving our arms and legs up and down, creating perfect snow angels.

We woke Mom up. She put on her full-length Tenuki fur coat and came outside with us. She had never seen a snow angel. Had never made one. We flung her into the whiteness to join our battalion. For an hour that's what we were: our own Night Watchmen, hand in hand, creating snow angels along the entire perimeter of our house to guard, keep and bless our home.

JANUARY 4, 1991

My mother has never hid her fear very well or her selfishness for that matter. I am not sure which is born from the other. I think most times my mother is just simply in over her head. Most of my images of her during this time are of her dressed in a suit, clutching her Louis Vuitton bag, high-heels clicking on tile leaving a perfumed cloud of Guerlain's Shalimar in her wake as she walks out the door to work.

I don't think she ever wanted to work as much as she did. I don't think she ever intended to be a career woman. I think once she and my father married, she wanted only to be a wife and a mother. But, that's not how life turned out for her. Now, the office to which she goes reluctantly has become her personal haven. She gets to leave. I am the one who stays. My brother and I stay. Somehow I think we see more than my mother. She is at work. Taking care of us in a different way. In the way she can, protecting our future. She sure as hell wasn't protecting our present.

Tonight, both fear and selfishness, these ugly twins, were worn on her sleeve as she chased me from room to room screaming.

"I GOT A MAMMOGRAM TODAY! DON'T YOU CARE HOW I AM? DOESN'T ANYONE CARE HOW I AM?"

I ran to my room to pack. Where I was going I had no idea. Anywhere.

Anywhere but here.

A hairbrush flew past my head. She tugged at my arms crying (apparently, one need not be an Italian matriarch to pull it off) begging me not to leave. I recalled at once where I had seen the look on her face before: in the basement, with my grandfather, ten years ago. It was more frantic now, more hysterical, unhinged.

She knew she was losing.

"Everyone asks how Matt is. No one asks how I am!" She yelled at me.

"You're not dying, Mom. He is." I screamed back.

"He's not dying until I say he can die. Your father and I have always checked in with each other before we did anything that would affect the family. He'll do as I say."

I am not kidding. She really said that.

She really thought she could control his illness. That she could love him to wellness. That she was so strong, so powerful that if she and she alone worked hard enough, took care of him long enough, better and more fiercely, he would not die.

"He cannot die." She said.

"He simply cannot die *because* I love him."

It was the first time I had ever seen my mother's face not paralyzed with fear. It was the first time in all of this, in this whole ordeal that her voice did not quiver, but was strong, solid. It was the first time I saw her eyes soften and shine with not tears of loss, but tears of the joy and love she had known with my father. It was the first time I saw my mother as my father's lover, as his friend, as his life. It was the first time I understood that what she was about to lose was something I hoped I would one day feel.

It was the only time I have ever seen my mother's love so clearly.

"I think, Mom, that you should reverse that. He can die *because* you love him." It was the only thing that came to my mind to say.

She then did something that at once, scared, confused and thrilled me.

She held me. Closely she held me and smoothed my hair with her right hand. She had not done that since I was a child. The memory returned and like that child I snuggled in closer, closer still, 'til I lay in her lap and cried.

I could have cried for my father, but I didn't. I could have cried for my brother who would grow up to become a man without the guidance of one, but I didn't. I could have cried for my mother, but that would have taken too long.

Instead, I cried for myself. I cried for being so tired at twenty-one years old, for having to be a grown-up for so long, for having to parent my parents and mother my brother. For foreseeing my father's death ten years before on the day I became ageless and old. For feeling sick every time I left his room because the smell of the room and the sound of his rattling breath made me want to retch. For wanting to run away every time I heard his cry: the screaming, piercing, shrill like a police car or an ambulance, signifying help or rescue. But there is no help, no rescue from this. Not for me. I cannot be rescued from myself, from my fucking obligations, from my father's smell, his screams or the rattle in his lungs as every organ in his body dies before him.

Mostly I cry because earlier today, while I was cleaning up around my father's bed, he caught my eye with a lucidity and clarity that simultaneously startled and thrilled me. In this moment, I saw him. I saw my old dad, my alive dad, my well dad. With all the energy he could muster, he reached behind him with his right hand, his good hand and pulled the pillow from under his head. He placed it over his face and pushed down. He then removed the pillow, looked at me again and pointed to me to do the same thing.

My father was asking me to kill him.

For a second I actually thought about it. Then was shocked out of my euthanasic trance by the actual reality of this surreal request.

"Easy for you to say." I said.

"You will die," I said. " But I will have to live with that my entire life and I won't be able to so I might as well die with you."

He turned away from me. I don't know what was worse, his disappointment with me, my disappointment with myself for not doing what my father asked of me or his shame in asking his daughter to do the unimaginable.

Fucking kill me now.

And, so I cry.

I cry. I cry. I cry. Guiltily, I cry hoping my father,   143 somewhere in between here and there, in between the clear and the fog, in his living purgatory, will recognize his child's plea not only for comfort, but also for forgiveness.

JANUARY 10, 1991

It is 11 PM. It is very dark outside. The moon hangs overhead like a solitary eye keeping an ever-careful vigil over us. I am driving in my car. My headlights together with the moonlight illuminate the empty streets and dark houses. There is a figure dressed in white slowly moving toward me in the middle of the road. I stop the car. It turns its ghostly head to me. It's eyes flash in the brightness of the headlights. It does not shield its eyes from the glare, but stares straight ahead as if entranced. It is a man. A hospital gown falls loosely off his shoulders. He looks around, his arms and hands held upward beseeching something only he sees. He looks at me in question, in confusion.

"Help me find my way. I cannot find my way. I hear them. They are calling for me, but I cannot find them. I need to go now." The man asks of me.

"Are you lost, Daddy?"

He holds out his hands to me. Together we walk down the road looking for the faceless voices that call to him. I feel like a mother walking her child to school, knowing I will never pick him up. We walk until I realize I am walking alone. In my hand is a crumpled white hospital gown, its strings from the shoulders trail behind me on the ground.

I do not feel sad. I do not feel frightened.

I feel happy. For in this vision while I drive to 7-11 for a pack of cigarettes, I know my father has found his way home.

JANUARY 11, 1991

I called my manager. I told her I would be booking-out the next week as my father would die this weekend.

144   "How can you know that?" She asked me.

"He showed me."

JANUARY 12, 1991

We waited.

Chapter Thirteen

"Get down into your Kiva
That place inside us all
Where the sound of Life passing
Is a beating heart."

"The Good Red Road"
Ned Farr

APRIL 1982

We will long remember Friday, April 16th 1982 as our 16th wedding anniversary. More than that it will be remembered as a new beginning. Linda left work about noon for home and puttered around, checking and rechecking the list of things we needed to complete the house in Montauk. I left work at about three. We were very excited about going out to the house to "finish it," to celebrate our anniversary. The children were taken care of. When I got home, all of the finishing touches were lying in the driveway, waiting to be loaded into the wagon. The rug padding, the new sink sprayer, the potpourri to scent the house, the new candles and candleholders, the white marble chips to complete the fireplace base and my notes, typewriter and paper for this story.

On the way out, we picked up a bunch of daisies for Linda, an azalea plant for our neighbors, who have been so kind to us, two lobsters for our special dinner and a bottle of champagne. We also stopped at a pottery store in East Hampton to purchase two beautifully sculptured wooden butterflies that we had seen the week before. This was to be our anniversary gift to each other.

We arrived, put everything in its place and sat down to dinner. We talked about how far we had come and how much had happened. It was a year and six months, almost to the day, since my operation and we toasted with champagne. Soft music played in the background and the fireplace shed a beautiful light. I hung *our gift, the butterflies, in just the right spot.*

What is the old saying? —"Butterflies are free" – hopefully, so are we. We love each other; things seem to be back on track again. Life is good. But you can't go through an experience like we did without learning something. We are still affected by our environment and are vitally aware of our obligations, financial problems, material possessions and all the day-to-day frustrations and screw ups at work and home. But they just don't have the same importance anymore. Only life and those I love are important to me. I'm grateful for them every day. As Ransohoff said, "There are no guarantees." Knowing this is a gift and has made it all worthwhile.

AUGUST 1982

I awoke one morning and said, "I've had enough!" The family business was no longer a challenge. I was restless and yearning for something more. I am totally convinced that coming back from brain surgery gave me the confidence to finally leave the business. I didn't know what I was going to do. I had lots of contacts in both acting and business and more importantly, I had Linda's full support.

SEPTEMBER 16, 1982

I had an appointment with Ransohoff for my two-year post surgery CAT scan checkup.

We arrived at 11 AM for our scheduled appointment. They were behind schedule and so we were told to come back at 2:30. Linda thought, "Is this an omen?" I felt better than I ever had, but Linda began to feel all those old emotions resurrecting themselves. They had been waiting patiently.

We took the opportunity to have lunch with Jon.

When we returned to NYU Medical Center, they told us my scan was now moved to 4:30. I called Sue, Ransohoff's secretary. She said, "We'll be here," in a groggy voice.

My name was finally called. I walked in confidently, leaving Linda, a bag of nerves, outside.

After I was given my contrast solution, I went outside to make sure Linda was all right. I found her sitting in a corner, legs crossed, top leg going a mile a minute. Just like old times.

I returned to the scanner room and watched as the technician scanned the person ahead of me. Then it was my turn. By this time I just wanted to get in and out as fast as possible. After she finished, I told her Ransohoff was waiting for the results and could she please speed it up. I watched as my scan appeared on the video display. I saw no tumor. But what did I know? After they were developed, she gave them to me and I took them out to show Linda on our way up to Ransohoff's office. She didn't want to see them until Ransohoff did. Superstition?

We arrived at his office and as usual it was still crowded. It was obvious something was wrong with Sue. Papers and files were strewn all over the place, where normally she was as fastidious as Ransohoff. Another omen?

He came out and asked Sue who was next. She sort of fished through the messy files, held her head and started mumbling. (We later found out she had the flu and was heavily medicated. Trooper that she is, she continued working.) It was then that we noticed something had changed in Ransohoff. Where he once would have screamed at her, he tried to help her. There was softness about him that we had never seen before. He called in the next patient and winked when he saw me. We were alone in his office, just Linda, Sue and myself. Since my file was on the counter with the others, I walked over and picked it up. I was reading it when Ransohoff came out and said, "I guess you're next." We went into his inner office: Still two packs of cigarettes on his desk. One, as yet, not opened. I handed him my scans and my file. He put the scans up against the backlight to compare them to last years.

"These are super," he said. "No tumor, a little thickening between the lobes... but that's normal scar tissue. I don't have to see you for three years."

_WE WERE ECSTATIC!_

I asked about reducing my medication. He replied, "No fits, no seizures? Why play around with it and go through it all again. It's no big deal."

I had to agree.

I told him I read the file because I was doing a story about my surgery and he was featured. He smiled a coy grin and said, "That's okay. You know I've been featured before. You're not the first."

"Shainberg's book?" I asked.

"Yeah," he replied. "It's caused me a lot of problems. Because of it I'm in the midst of a divorce, living with a 26-year-old whom I'll probably marry and am the happiest I've ever been. Imagine that? Forty years difference!"

"Good for you." I said.

"You look terrific. It must agree with you." Linda added.

"What the hell. My mother said you only live twice." Dr. Ransohoff joked as he extended his arm out with his hand showing the victory sign.

We had to agree: for hadn't he just given us our second lives?

As we sat in La Moal, where it had all began; we had come full circle. We put our past behind us and toasted to a new beginning. One filled with optimism, uncertainty and most importantly…love.

Alan Alda

August 15, 1983

Dear Mr. Coppola,

Thank you for sending me a
copy of "You Only Live Twice."
It must have been a very difficult
time in your life and I can
understand your wanting to write
about it.

I'm sorry to say, though, that
I'm so over committed right now
with work and commitments extending
very far into the future that I'm
not able to involve myself in
another project.

I know how hard it is to get
something off the ground - and I
realize that this story is important
to you personally, so I wish you
great good luck in getting it
produced.

Sincerely,

Alan Alda

September 13, 1983

Dear Alicia,

I would just like to relate a tale to you about a 38 year old married man with two children, who suddenly found himself, by his own doing, out of work with no income.

He was frieghtened, scarred and unsure about what he had done, and he knew he could never go back, under any circumstances.

Fortunately, his wife was very proud of what he had done and could support the family on her income alone, until he found new employment.

So he made up his resumes and started to send them out to people in his related industry. He waited for all the job offers, and he waited and waited! They never came in. Every ad he answered was a very nice rejection or a no response at all. Then he decided, with his wife, to do something he always wanted to do. Thorough planning and discipline through some very tight times he and they set out on this new venture. They had to adjust and accomodate thier lifestyle because this new venture started out paying ZERO. Moreover, he really didn't know anything about what he was doing so he had to put in long hours of retraining, learning new skills, studying new techniques. He had to discipline himself, draw on his fortitude and self motivation.

Well he is still doing that. Every day when he gets up in the morning he says, "I've got to conquor this day and do a little better than yesterday, for if I don't my life will be meaningless."

His wife gets up in the morning and says the same thing, and together they go on hoping for a better future.

They have two beautiful children who bring them great pride and joy, and who they love more than anything in the world. They want the best for them. If the best means sending them off to a school that will give them the advantages that they never had, even though it means initial unhappiness for both parents and children, then that's the way it has to be. It is because we love them so dearly that we want the best for them.

Please stick it out for the year, I promise you , you won't be sorry.

Love
Dad

Chapter Fourteen

"To-day, the road all runners come,
Shoulder-high we bring you home,
And set you at your threshold down,
Townsman of a stiller town."

To An Athlete Dying Young
A.E Houseman[8]

JANUARY 13, 1991

Sunday. 11:41 AM
Dad died this morning.

George Winston's *December,* the CD we had played for him for the past month to soothe and comfort him with its soft piano melodies, played in the background.

I woke, got out of bed, and went into his room as I have done every day since he came home from the hospital that last final time to say, "Hello I love you." I sat for a bit, listening quietly to his labored breathing and saw how pale and wax like he looked. He looked like a wax replica of himself. Like the kind one would see at the Hollywood Wax Museum. He did not look like my father. I left his room to go into the kitchen to call Ned. He was to come out for a visit today, but suddenly I did not think it was a good idea. Just as I was saying hello into the phone, my mother came into the kitchen, ordered me to hang up the phone and very calmly and plainly said "your daddy's dead."

The walk back into his room should have taken no more than a few seconds. Instead it seemed to take an hour. I could not help but berate myself with each step: Why wasn't I there? Right goddamned there? I'd seen everything else, been there for everything else, why not this? I felt shame; shame for ever wanting to be anywhere else. Because with my final step, there was the only place I really wanted to be.

I found a sturdy place to stand. Against the closet door I felt my knees buckle but the door somehow held my weight. Matthew sat, head in his hands on the ottoman beside the bed. Mom knelt beside Dad, stroking his hair.

We should have been prepared for this. Medically speaking we were. But during all of this, during the wait for this moment, we never said goodbye. I never said goodbye. I said other things, many, many other things. But never once did I say the words *goodbye*. If he had just dropped dead of a heart attack or been hit by a bus, I wouldn't have been able to say goodbye. Why, with all the chances, all the months leading up to this moment did I not say the most obvious words? Why had they eluded me? I think the answer is simple: that simple phrase became a four-letter word, its utterance forbidden.

My mother tried to get his ring off his finger. She tugged and pulled, every movement caused my father's body to rise and fall, rise and fall. Just like the past ten years, he rose above and fell below. In an action that was strangely sexual and therefore unwelcome to me, she licked his finger and straddled his body, tugging on his left ring finger. It came off. A souvenir of the widow's honeymoon she was about to embark upon.

I laughed. I laughed like I hadn't laughed in years. I laughed from shock, denial and fear. I laughed until my sides ached and my stomach revolted and I laughed until I couldn't laugh anymore.

Matthew got up from the ottoman, touched Dad's face and bent down to say something in his ear that I never heard. It was not meant for me to hear. He straightened up, turned around and never again set foot in that room. I left the safety of my closet door and lay next to my father. I felt about his gown for evidence of a pocket. I thought I could climb in and take the journey with him so he wouldn't ever be alone again. For all the times I feared coming into this room, I wanted to give myself over to him completely. I wanted to be with him like I used to be, like we used to be, uncomplicated, with no prodding and poking, no pin pricks from needles searching for veins, no catheters, no morphine drips, no hospice nurses shuffling about uselessly, no bed sores, no shit stains, no tears, no fear, no fear, no fear. I wanted him to carry me away with him like he did before he cast me into my mother to be born to see all of this.

There was no pocket. Only strings holding up his gown, taunting me to hang myself.

My mother asked me to leave the room, to leave them alone.

As I left the room, the morbid Magi appeared: Doctor, Nurse and Hearse Driver. The former two were there for us. They couldn't help my father any more. The latter, the coachman, he was there for my father.

I asked him to not cover my father's face with the sheet. I thought as they drove through town, my father might want a last look around. I also told him to put my father's favorite Jazz station on the radio. He nodded, went into the room, rolled Dad out on a stretcher, out the door and out of my sight. The neighbors, who were home, finally came out of their houses and with respect, stood silently, as if in prayer, as my father was driven by. A sad parade if ever there was.

The house was silent. There was nothing left to do. There was no howling, no sirens, and no noise. It was as quiet as a tomb: an empty tomb.

It had recently been raided.

I made phone calls. I called Ned. I needed Ned. I needed him like I needed to breathe. I inhaled when I called him and held it until he arrived.

We drove to the beach. My father's beach. The one Matthew and I took him two weeks before, after his blood tests. I got out of the car. Ned followed me. I exhaled. Loudly and violently, I exhaled and pummeled Ned and screamed and choked and gasped and yelled and everything, everything I had felt being held up by the closet door came tumbling down and I crumbled with it, with only Ned to hold me up. I don't know how long we stood there. I don't know how long Ned 157 held me, but I know this: in those moments, Ned became the only person in the world, up until that point in my life, who had ever seen me broken. Truly, unalterably, broken.

I remembered the knife of so long ago. I remembered my young image, distorted and cold. I remembered the pain I was in at the time. It was nothing like I felt at this moment. No knife could have cut me deeper than this.

JANUARY 14, 1991

We drove through town. We drove to the funeral parlor. The father of one of Matthew's friends owned it. When we arrived, my mother asked if she could see my father. The director said no, he didn't think that was a good idea. She then asked for a lock of hair from dad's beard.

He agreed to that.

My father was to be cremated. He did not want to be buried. He wanted his ashes to be scattered in the ocean in Montauk. Apparently, that did not go over well with the Italians. They don't like their people being scattered to the wind, because then there is no place to visit. No headstone to mark the life of the one who has passed. No Sunday afternoon visit to the cemetery to "pay their respects." There is nothing to remind them, it is as if the person who died never existed at all. All has been erased. Personally, I think they don't like cremation because they can't hurl themselves on the casket and wail inconsolably. They like that, makes them feel like they put in a good day of mourning. He was to be slid into an oven like a pizza and burnt. Flames would dance around him, engulf him and consume him leaving nothing of the man but ash.

Ash and bone.

His parents carried him home forty-eight years ago in a soft blue baby blanket, a small bouncing boy bundle of flesh and blood.

We carried him home in a small white shiny box of ash and bone.

*****

My father had it his way and we held a service at The Old First Presbyterian Church in Huntington. It was a full house. I do not recall much of the day, except that when I spoke at the podium, reciting one of my father's favorite poem's, A.E. Houseman's *To An Athlete Dying Young*, I saw many eyes glistening back at me. I think everyone in the room knew what we had lost.

Food and drink make people feel alive. It is comforting. After a funeral, people need to feel together and they need to feel alive. Everyone came back to our house afterwards. One of my roommates from Kent (the one whose father was gone, not dead, just gone,) came to the service and back to the house. It was incredibly kind of her. She really loved my father and he her. It was actually a very nice party. My uncle played the piano and we danced. He played "Softly As I Leave You" for my mother while she sat on the piano bench and leaned against him. We drank wine, we talked, we laughed, and we actually had a good time. The phone rang. I answered it.

A man's voice greeted me," Hi Alicia."

"Who's speaking?" I asked.

"I'll give you a hint…we used to spend a lot of time together."

"Look, my father just died, we are having his memorial right now, I am in no mood for games. Who is this?" I asked again.

"Alicia," said the voice, only this time the voice was softer and I knew who it was. Rather, my heart knew. "It's me, Aiden and I just heard. I am sorry. I always loved your father. He was always supportive of me, of us."

It had been so long. So long since we had spoken last. I think it had been when we had finally broken up during my sophomore year of NYU. Every memory of our time flooded my mind and wanting to say so much to him, I very simply thanked him for calling and hung up. I think sometimes when you have been especially close to someone and have gone through something painful his or her very presence hurts. The very sight or sound of them becomes a reminder and therefore unbearable. This was the case with Aiden. This was the case with the majority of the people who came to my father's memorial. I never wanted to see them again.

Lucky for me, I didn't have to. My mother immediately sold our house in Huntington and moved to Montauk. Prior to my father's final battle, my mother and he began construction on our house in Montauk. I am not sure whether it was out of hope for a future together or in prayer for any kind of future alone, but my mother kept the construction going all throughout what was my father's last year. What was their little dream cottage on the water is now my mother's bedroom! She added on to what was already there and created a magnificent home...perhaps she felt that if she were to have a new life, she'd need a new house. I think my father would have really loved it for I am sure it was built as testament to him.

My brother went back to UVM in a valiant attempt to finish what he started and I took a little house in Centerport, close to our childhood home so that when Matthew came home from school, he would be close to his friends. Nice as that sounds, that is not the only reason I stayed in Long Island. I stayed because I was not ready to go back to the city. I could work there and ironically, for I truly believe my father orchestrated it, shortly after his death, I began what would turn out to be a three-year stint on a soap opera, NBC's *Another World*, in Brooklyn. I was enormously grateful for the many hours of work that kept me quite busy. They worked me 5 days a week, roughly 12-13 hours daily. I was grateful beyond belief.

I had an incredible storyline and was given the gift of working with some of the show's greatest actors. I was able to shove down deep the remnants of the recent past and be someone else for the majority of the day. I honestly don't know where I did my best work, on or off the set. The actors and crew of *Another World* became my family. They saw me through much of my grief and never, not once in my three years on that show, did I not have an open pair of arms to fold into. I have often said and shall always believe that Linda Dano, who played Felicia Gallant on the show and my character's mother, picked up raising me, where my own mother treading the waters of her own grief, left off. To this day, Linda is my "mama." Always will be. Also, I was in Brooklyn, walking the streets where my father grew up. Where he became a young man, was in a sense where I was becoming a young woman. Being close to his past helped me find my present.

But to live there, I was not ready to do. I was not ready to pack up the past six months into a cardboard box from the deli and shove it into a closet with the rest of my stuff. I didn't want to go back to the life I had before, because I didn't really remember who I was before. It was a foggy time for me. I needed time for the mist to lift. Quite simply, I needed time to heal. My little cottage became my quarter-life convalescent home.

It's funny. My little cottage was in Centerport, the town my father grew up in, down the street in fact from his childhood home where my grandparents still lived. It was also up the street from his beach, the one Matthew and I took him to just weeks before he died and where we heard the shutter clicking in his heart snapping picture after picture to keep him company on his journey. It was also the beach I walked, paced rather, to find the strength to say goodbye to the past and seek the grace to face my future. It was the beach where I grew up, where Ned became my spine and where I prayed I could begin to hopefully and finally let go.

And perhaps, get gracefully gone.

# Epilogue 2013

"Well... we have passed... we are chronicle now to the eerie,
Curious metal from meteors that failed in the sky:
Earth-born the tireless is stretched by the water, quite weary,
Close to this un-understandable changeling that's I...
Fear is the echo we traced to Security's daughter:
Now we are faces and voices.... and less, too soon,
Whispering half-love over the lilt of the water...
Youth the penny that bought delight of the moon."

This Side Of Paradise
F. Scott Fitzgerald[9]

Pink cashmere embraces her.
Shrouding her like a hug from God.
Blushing faintly in answer
To my question,
She leaves the room to decide
If she will lie.
She won't. Only mothers lie.
This mother is a woman first
And women never lie to their children.
We were two little people
My brother and I
Raised to stand alone.
        "Would you rather I lie?"
She would question in response to our own.
They were innocent, shocking
And later as life died on...for safety;
        "Where do babies come from?"
        "What is a blow job?"
        "Will Nana die from Alzheimer's?"
The genesis of our maturity:
One eleven, one seven
We were force fed the apple.
        "What is brain cancer?"
        Can we catch it?"
        "Will daddy die?"

We chewed.
Not permitted to purge,
We swallowed.
A nod or shake of her proud beige mane
That matched her champagne colored Porsche
Would answer.
Neither to protect
Nor to educate
Her truth hid us from darkness
And untimely, we aged.
      "Would you rather I lie?"
It was a question
Born of maternal duty
Yet nurtured in insecurity.
An answer of "yes" meant
She walked alone.
Tugging on the dead man's finger
We watched, my brother and I
Her steal the ring
Signifying widowhood.
Woman turned wife
Turned mother
Turned widow
Turned shadow.
A broken shell
Of a woman first.
Ebullient eyes filmed over
With the cataract of the catatonic.
And, like Fitzgerald's words
Gave way to silent cigarettes,
She ceased searching for the light.
Finding nothing
But cool sand beneath her feet
And ocean air salty in her mouth

She tasted the sweetness of strength.
And, blinded by herself, he came.
Shadow turned widow
Turned woman
Turned wife once more.
>"Are you ready for this?"
>"What about dad?"
>"What about us?"
>"Would you rather I lie?"
As champagne was poured
And flowers arranged
As guests tenderly arrived
As if treading on daddy's grave
We wished she would.

But then the phone call came.
It always does.
We listened, my brother and I
But did not hear.
>"Chronic leukemia...will he die?"
Reining her tears on a choke chain
Barring her cries
Posturing strength
She straightens and sighs
>"If you don't mind, I think I'll lie."

Alicia Coppola - 1994

I recall all the things I felt growing up. My palms still tingle at the thought of holding that knife in my twelve-year old bedroom so long ago. My heart breaks for the girl who felt left out of the crowd, who struggled so hard just to be liked, to fit in. I feel so sad for the young woman in college who couldn't just enjoy the hell out of every new experience she had instead of worrying every damn thing into the ground. I wish I could tell her now to relax, to have patience with herself. I wish I could scream at her: "STOP TRYING SO FUCKING HARD TO PLEASE EVERYONE!!!!!!!! PLEASE YOURSELF!!!!!" I wish she would understand that if she did just that, the rest would follow. She would be all right. My heart aches in apology for the men who wanted nothing more than to see me through my troubles and got absolutely nothing in return. I remember them well and kindly. They may not have known the extent to which they helped me. So just in case… Thank you. I am filled with gratitude.

I also feel great sadness for my mother, who went through so much and then God bless her, went through it all again...

His name was Olivier.

Olivier rode into our lives in a big, blue van. He rode in by way of Washington State where he learned English as a cook at "TGIF." He learned English so he could tell his newborn son about his history. He spoke to his son in French so he could learn the language of his people. He spoke to his son of royalty, of the family to which he was born a Baron. Born son of a Baron, Grandson of the Marquis and Countess. He stayed in Washington until his son was five, old enough, Olivier felt, to understand his heritage and old enough to know his father. When Olivier felt confident of his standing in his son's life, as he was no longer married to his son's mother, he went east, east to East Hampton, New York, to live in one room of his Uncle's home. It was a far cry from the palace in which he had grown in Normandy. Further still from the wealth and opulence accorded to the bloodline of his family -- Napoleon on his mother's side and Louis XIV on his father's.

But that was all ok with him.

His son knew who he was. His son spoke French fluently. Olivier spoke English not so fluently but enough to be understood charmingly as only the French can be and he was seeking a new life away from his family and their royal obligations and bullshit pomp and circumstance, to make a life on his own terms.

My mother and I met him Christmas Eve 1994. It was a party her friend the painter was throwing for, I believe, just this purpose.

We sat on a couch by the fireplace. Olivier, short, slight of build, with a hooked nose and curly black hair, handsome as only a French man can be, sat opposite us, staring at my mother.

"That man is looking at you." I whispered.

"Who?" She asked.

"The man over there...He looks like he's opened an early Christmas present."

She laughed, pooh-poohed me and decided it was time to leave.

Not to be ignored, as we were leaving, I said it again. *"That man was looking at you."*

She dismissed me, 'Don't be ridiculous. He was probably looking at you.'

I know when a man is looking at me. Believe me, this

one was not.

We got into the car. But not before I spied Olivier outside the house watching as we drove off.

He was laughing. He had heard every word.

The next day, a bouquet of wild flowers arrived at the shop where my mother had started working. She had re-invented herself into a seemingly carefree bohemian type, living on the water in Montauk, working for fun, not money, in a boutique on East Hampton's fashionable Main St. Gone were the corporate days of 9-5. Gone were her suits and high heels and gone were the businesses that had always taken her away from us. She wore jeans and sweaters now, grew out her hair and sold funky art and high-end ceramics to the Hampton's wealthy elite.

The bouquet began their courtship. It was brief, yet powerful to hear her tell it. One day my mother was a widow, the next, she was living in sin. He moved in. She had the house on the water. He had the talents of a Renaissance man: he was chef, refinisher of fine antiques and could repair a Louis XIV chair so that no one, not even Ol' Louie himself, could ever tell the difference. She believed my father sent Olivier to her. She believed they had actually met years before, in another time, another life, when she and my father were honeymooning in Antigua. She recalled a certain curly haired someone who had watched her and my father as they boarded a boat to take them deep sea diving. She believed Olivier was that certain someone. She believed what she wanted to believe, despite what my brother and I thought, despite what anyone thought and good for her.

He was, as I would to come to believe myself, a good man. I came to have a great respect and a deep affection for him. He was an honest, hardworking man, not out to scam the vulnerable widow-of-a-certain-age, who was more well-off than he, but start a life with the woman he loved, the woman who he chose in a glance, all those years ago. He loved her and she, him. She was over the moon, a second chance at

168

happiness and a second chance at life. A gift was wrapped and placed before her and she eagerly, like a child on Christmas morning, opened it.

They married. But not before Olivier, feeling a bit under the weather went to see the doctor. The test results were inconclusive yet foreboding.

"What do I tell him? What should we do?" My mother asked the doctor.

"Tell him nothing, do nothing. Get married. Call me after."

This was his sage advice.

She did as she was told. She told Olivier nothing and walked down the aisle of her upper deck looking out on the water to her brand spanking new husband not knowing what was wrong with him.

"I do. Until death us do part. I do."

She did it. God Bless and damn her. She actually did it.

More tests were done and Olivier was told he had Leukemia. Tests upon tests, hospital stays here and abroad in France where treatments were free and did not have to be approved by the FDA, the arsenal of the diseased re-entered our lives and the beat went on.

And on.

And on.

Until the morning of the phone call, my mother summoning me home to do what we all knew she couldn't do alone. Until the whirring of the machine, that kept Olivier alive even after he died. The machine I had to unplug. He had waited for me. He knew, that French son of a baron bitch knew I'd be the one to do this thing. I'd be the one to free him. I'd be the one to take care of everything that now had to be taken care of. He knew I'd do it just like he'd want, like he would do it, cleanly and swiftly. He knew I'd do it cold. Because I knew it cold. Knew it by heart. He knew I'd take care of my mother just like I always had because he knew she'd never be able to do any of it herself. After all, I knew my role. I'd played it before. I fell into it like a second skin, like I never wrapped the production the first time.

169

I was good at it.

Since I was twelve I feel like I have walked the red carpet to the premieres of my mother's dramas, not as the star, but as the supporting player who gets no applause even though she's carried the show. Because in this show, up until now, I have felt that the stars were my mother and her husbands. Maybe they were. Or maybe the stars of this show were the white, shiny boxes of ash that seemed to encapsulate our lives. Their contents were not alone, for my mother, brother and I, although never licked by the heat, I think we too went up in the smoke and reside within its whiteness.

*****

I cannot say that I have had a trouble free relationship with my mother. It has been at times down right turbulent. I cannot say that I have completely forgiven her for not protecting my brother and I both as children while our father died and as young adults as Olivier succumbed. I cannot say that I honestly ever felt mothered. I felt somewhat guided and befriended by her presence, but never fully mothered. What I can say is that after years -- and I do mean years -- of therapy, I understand her. I understand my mother. Wow. That's a loaded statement. I think it's quite simple: she could not be alone with the knowledge that her loves were dying, that her life was so drastically changing without her consent. So she clung to my brother and I like life preservers, holding herself up at the same time as she pushed us under. I don't think she ever meant to do Matthew and I harm, she just needed to float.

Ok. Ok.

My mother now, trying to look at the bright side of her life, always says how lucky she has been in her life to have known not one, but *two* great loves. (She is also a Baroness for Christ sakes! How many seventy-year old American broads can say that? Not many I'll tell you!) Most people never even find one. I believe that she was lucky to have had such love. I know she did the best she could do for us and was simply and terribly, a loving woman struck by shitty luck. I know... lucky and unlucky all at the same time. There's the rub. I hope that I am never in her position and pray I never know an eighth of what's she forgotten. I actually feel in some ways that I now have the mother I have always wanted. At times of despair, she is still the person I call when I need to talk, when I need someone to lean on. She has seen me through much and has never judged me. Perhaps because she herself has been judged. She is incredibly supportive of my brother and I. She has never wavered in her belief in us and is very generous of spirit. I have great respect for her, for the strength she possesses, I love her dearly and I applaud the life and happiness she has found for herself.

I feel regret at times for my brother, Matthew who floundered for many years. I feel sorry for the boy who got stuck between my mother and I. I feel sorry that he had to grow up with out the guidance of a father. I feel sorry that I couldn't protect him more. Though at other times I am amazed that I was able to protect him as much as I did.

The other day I was telling him about the time I held his hand and walked him across the golf course of the country club to our grandparent's house. My mother was busy with my father and I just wanted to get Matthew out of the house. I didn't drive yet, that came a few months later, so we walked. He told me he didn't remember any of it. There is a lot he doesn't remember. So that's good. That is good. I can be gentle with myself now, after all, I was just a twelve-year old girl.

I do take great pride in that he is now, just now, finding himself and his life away from the diseased drama of our childhood. He channeled his experience into a film called "fresh cut grass." It is the story of a boy, graduating from college with a degree in pot smoking and Lacrosse, who struggles to find himself after the loss of his father. The main character, Zach, learns life lessons from the gardeners he works with for the summer after he graduates. "You pick a point on the lawn," they tell him. "If you don't pick the point, you'll just go around and171 around in circles. As long as you keep your eye on the point, you'll always go in a straight line."

It may have taken him some time going in circles, but Matthew has picked his point and he is on that straight line. He lives in California, pursing his dream of writing and directing and at this writing is in a loving relationship with a girl he dated in college and is the father of two beautiful little girls.

I too, like my mother, have found great love. I have found four great loves: my husband and my daughters. It took me a long time to find them and most of that time was hard, but so well worth the journey. Like my brother, I, too, struggled going around and around in circles. But I finally picked the right point when I met my husband Anthony.

That happened in 1994. He was dating my best friend (not to be confused with the "best friend" from childhood) at the time and I was dating a writer/director, with whom I felt I might have a future. Anthony tells a story about being in an Upper West Side restaurant and seeing a girl walk by the bar. Lots of girls walked by him, still do actually, he's quite fetching. He says that seeing that girl from across the proverbial crowded restaurant impacted him in a unique and profound way and he wondered how he could ever find her again as she slipped out into the night with her friends. Little did he know, a few weeks later my best friend, his girlfriend would introduce him to that girl.

Me.

We met and we knew, but what we knew we weren't exactly sure. (Before you adorn me with the Scarlet A and call me a homewrecker or in our case, an apartment wrecker, as fate would have it, he and she ended their relationship for their own reasons. She and I later ended our friendship for our own reasons. All of these reasons happened way before the following occurred. It was all on the up and up, copasetic if you will.)

Anthony and I became friendly but our lives took us in different directions until 1997.

During 1994-1997 I was back and forth to LA for work. It

was a lot of travel and though it pained me to do, since I missed (still do!) NY and my life there, I finally made the permanent move to LA in 1997. I had a hard time in LA at first. It was a very different life than the life I was living in NY. I felt very insulated and alone in LA. I was living around auditions and work and not much else. Without my father to take care of or working my ass off on the Soap, I had a lot of time on my hands and that for me equals anxiety and sadness. I felt like I was waiting to live my life, but something was missing. The key ingredient to my happiness eluded me. Where in NY I felt alive and full, in LA, I felt sad and empty. I had very few friends and my Writer/Director was back in NY.

Prior to my Writer/Director, I was dating an actor who was also on *Another World*. This relationship was the first serious one I had since Aiden. This was important. It made me feel not so broken. I had true and strong feelings for my Actor. I wasn't using him as a filling station. For the first time since Aiden, I felt like I was actually filling someone else. I felt as if I was contributing to someone else's happiness and that in turn made me happy. This relationship lasted for a good length of my time on the show.

He was a wonderful Band-Aid. He helped me bridge the profound sadness of my father's death to the excitement and new happiness of the life I was starting to have.

I felt alive and like everything was going to be A-Ok! We even apartment hunted together…a very bold and entrancing move. My Actor was cute, funny, and athletic and adored me until he went skiing in Colorado and found someone he adored more.

To say it crushed me would be an extreme miscarriage of an understatement.

I felt abandoned all over again and felt the death of my father all over again. It was my own emotionally and spiritually terrorizing version of the movie *Ground Hog's Day*. The panic, confusion and extreme sorrow I felt, when I became ageless and old at twelve years old and again during college after Aiden and I broke up and after my father died, washed over me again like a tidal wave and within it I completely drowned.

I was left. Alone. Again.

Breathe. Pray. Heal.

I had to start healing all over again.

Months later, I started to do just that with my Writer / Director. He came into my life at a beautifully perfect, yet terribly imperfect time. I really liked him. I wanted to play for keeps with him. I was determined that he be "The Other One" according to (I believe) Janis Joplin. ("I'm the ONE," she says and referring to her lover, "he's the Other One.")

But there was a problem.

Though I loved him, and I truly did, I was having a really hard time letting myself fall into him. Fall into trust, fall into ease, fall and be caught. I made my Writer/Director pay for the ghosts of my past, for my father's death, for my messy fucking life and for my Actor's trip to Colorado where he adored me less. Throughout our relationship I think I kept testing him sometimes unfairly, sometimes with cause, whether he failed or passed was irrelevant because somewhere deep inside me, though I knew and felt our feelings for each other were strong, I knew he would never catch me. Not because he didn't want to, but because I would never let him. I wouldn't let him because I felt like there would come a day where he would drop me. Not for anyone or anything else. He would one day just simply fumble and I would fall and I would break. I couldn't take that chance again. I just didn't trust. Not him, not anyone. I didn't trust that I wouldn't be left alone.

Again.

To this day, when I think of my Actor, I realize he was young and stupid and got in over his head. I was above his pay grade. He meant me no harm. I know that now.

When I think of my Writer/Director and I often do, it is always with warmth. If I am honest, when I am at my most alone and am my most quiet self, perhaps my thoughts of him, my Writer/Director, carry also the mere whisper of bittersweet loss.

*****

Anthony came out to LA during 1997 also for work and since he only knew me and one other friend he asked me to a play. I went but instead of going to the play we ate sushi and had our first kiss at the Bel Air Hotel. Three days later he moved in with me into my little West Hollywood apartment. In the three days between that first kiss and his moving in, I learned to fall and I let myself be caught. I trusted Anthony with a certainty that was as foreign to me as I was to it. Without knowing details of his life, I knew when I looked into his eyes that he had been hurt before in a very profound way. I knew in those first days, that he would never hurt me. He would never inflict on me what had been inflicted on him, what had already been so painfully inflicted on me. Anthony and I saved each other. I felt peaceful and happy. I knew my father had picked him, maybe in the same way he picked Olivier for my mother.

Anthony is so very much like my father in many ways. He is strong, thoughtful, sensitive, playful, and charming. He is a gentleman in the truest sense of that word. His gentleness is something I'd never felt before. Once I felt it, I knew I could not be with any one who was not gentle, who was not graceful, and who was not kind. Where one could find judgment, he finds compassion. He is humble, loyal and the smartest man I know.

He is Jesus. NO! I'm kidding. He just looks like him! A lot.

Sometimes I feel like my husband, God bless him, has raised me. He has helped me and guided me through my entire adult life. Everything I have become and all I have accomplished has been with him by my side. He is my barometer. He is my truth. He holds me carefully and with purpose. He is and will always be everything to me.

We eloped two years after he moved in.

My mother had planned a September 11th, 1999 wedding at her house in Montauk. She took me to Bergdorf 175

Goodman's to find a wedding dress and all the while I was trying to tell her it was not what I wanted. She refused to hear me. Finally over dinner that evening, Olivier said "Linda, listen to your daughter. She doesn't want this." My reasons for not wanting this wedding were twofold:

1. My memory harkened back to my twelve-year-old-self watching the "best friend" dance to "Daddy's Little Girl" which I assumed was a wedding band staple and I NEVER wanted to hear that dreadful ditty again in any way, shape or form. Just looking at a wedding band gave me the heebie-jeebies.

2. My prescience from when I was twelve had remained dormant within me for a few weeks later, Olivier took a turn for the worse and they needed to go to France for treatment.

While they were in France I wrote my mother a letter asking her to please let me have one day that was mine. One day that wasn't about dying. I just wanted to get married, Anthony and I, simply and quietly. She understood and she gave me that. I know it was hard for her, but that day was for me, for my future.

I needed to start it out right. In fact, the minister's assistant a lovely woman, whispered to me just as I was about to walk the aisle: "He is here, he is with you." I knew my father was there. I felt him and I knew he was proud.

*****

My daughters. Ah, my girls. Funny, having children was never something I was interested in. I don't think it ever actually occurred to me to have them. It wasn't until I met and married Anthony that I even began to think it might be something to do. Even then, I think I wanted to have a child more for Anthony than myself. He was the youngest of six and had way more experience than I and he wanted children. Actually, he wanted six. I told him to marry someone else when he told me that. Six? Can you imagine? Oy vey!

Mila is my first. She came into this world with a mission.

She is fierce and she is strong. She is as smart in her brain as she is in her heart. It's a combination both dangerous and fantastically rare. She tumbled down my walls and climbed back inside me. She moved from my womb into my heart where she lives. I know most parents say their children are their teachers. I am sure they are. Considering what I think of most parents I have met, I hope their children are teaching them.

I, of course, am a proud parent myself, but Mila is different for me. Mila gave me a gift when I gave birth...she gave me back myself. She gave me back the "me" I remember being before I turned twelve. She had to come to me so I could heal. So that I could know I was still the hopeful, trusting, fun, young person I was at twelve, before I became ageless and old. Because in loving her, in the simple process of mothering her, I mothered myself and I healed the little girl inside. I realize now I wasn't truly ok until Mila. I hid in my work, I hid in myself and I hid in Anthony. I hid, until Mila. The point that I picked in my own lawn all those years ago when Anthony and I chose one another, was always pointing towards Mila. Perhaps even more than finding myself, I had to know for once and for all that I was not my mother. That I do not mother like my mother. Mila gave me even that. In fact, one morning as I was driving a three-year old Mila to school, we came to a stoplight. I remember sighing aloud as I am wont to do. From the back seat, I heard this little voice say, "You'll be all right Mommy. You'll be ok."

I believed her. And, I was.

I am.

It was Mila who gave me the desire and the courage to have another baby. The desire was easy. The bravery, a breeze. The conception and holding on to the pregnancy bit...beyond difficult. It was years of trying and losing, of unbearable heartache. My life during this time was reduced to peeing on enough ovulation and pregnancy sticks that I might as well have peed on actual twenty-dollar bills. My life revolved around the two "fertile" weeks during every month. When news was good, the first three months, if we even made it that far, was full of secret bed stays and what Anthony calls 177 "circling the wagons." It was years of me shoving toilet paper wads up my vagina to see if my period had begun. Years of thinking something was wrong with me and years of doctor's visits that finally culminated in a few months of Clomid which made me bat-shit crazy, 2 IUI's and ultimately a round of InVitro Fertilization that ended badly. It was years of thousands upon thousands of dollars spent. *Jericho* money? Ha! Peed on it, shoved it up my vagina, injected it and swallowed it in hopes of a baby. All in hopes and years of crying so hard after Mila went to bed that I didn't think my poor husband could take another second of living with me.

Finally I had enough. I just stopped and resigned myself to mothering only Mila. I also resigned myself to one more round of In Vitro, thanks to my friend Christine, who said, "What the hell else do you have to do? Film and TV roles aren't going anywhere, your womb is. Come on! One more time!" So I gave it the last Hurrah, the last "college try," so to speak. I completely let go of any outcome and just lived my life. No more peeing on currency, no more sex for procreative purposes, no more hating all pregnant women I encountered and most important I considerably upped my daily wine consumption. It was then when Esmé Marlena made her entrance. What an entrance she made. The doctor thought we were having twins her levels were so high. She wanted to be here. She needed to be here. Esmé is the frosting. What Mila began, my Esmé completed. Or so I thought…

"We are not going to tie your tubes." My doctor says to me while beginning to stitch me up after my C-Section with Esmé. "Why do all that and add to your recovery when it took you so long to have this baby and the likelihood of your getting pregnant again is like being hit by lightning."

Famous last words… Five months later, as Esmé turns her head from my breast in disgust all of a sudden over my milk, I am perplexed. Weird I think. That night when I realize my period is four days late, I am concerned.

"You are weaning the baby anyway, perhaps it's just your

hormones going crazy and that's why your period is late." Says my paling-by-the-second husband.

"Just go get a test." I say. Again, I am back to peeing on currency. I don't even have to pee on this one. I just wave it near my vagina and it says positive! How can this be?! We were told I'd never get pregnant on our own again! We just spent the equivalent of a down payment on the 4-bedroom house we will now need to house the (gasp!) five of us on having Esmé! Well, pregnant I was and ten months later (The nine month thing? Big lie. Full forty weeks) meet Lightning... Miss Greta Helena arrives. She is happy, healthy, green eyed (!) and everything I never knew I wanted. I have three daughters.

I have three daughters!

I am reminded of a recurring dream I had as a child. I have only shared this with my husband and my therapist, it is black and white spotty images, like a spool of old film being shown on an old projector: a man in an aged and distressed leather jacket and a woman with a long graying braid in jeans and a T-shirt are photographed from the back. In between them are two dark haired little girls, one just a tiny bit taller than the other, holding hands. They are peaceful. They are a family. I never pictured *three* girls. In my dream there were only two.

I now know why... I always saw the image from the back. I never saw that Mila was always in front of us, as she should be.

Leading the way.

Leading *my* way.

So, I have it now...I have exactly what I have always wanted but never knew I could dream of. Like Willy Wonka says to Charlie and Grandpa Joe in the Wonkavator, "You do know what happens to the man who gets everything he ever wanted? He lives happily ever after."

Except the gray braid.

I neither braid nor am I gray.

Well, maybe a little. Gray that is.

Most of all, I feel really fortunate. I feel fortunate to

have had the experience with my father. I know it has changed me. I know that from age twelve on, I was never the same. I was never a carefree child, nor a wild teenager. Recently, I was at a birthday party for one of my daughter's classmates and a few of us moms were sitting around and talking. One of the mothers was recalling her crazy teenage days and looked to me as a kindred spirit to confirm that I too had a similar experience. "You remember what it was like," she said, "staying out late, drinking and hanging out with your friends."

"No," I said. "I was never like that. I never did any of that. I never had time to behave like a teenager."

I am not complaining, just stating a fact. I never got to do any of that stuff. I always tried to be good, to not add to my mother's already full plate. I know what that has cost me. I am aware of my pathology, like I said, years of therapy. I am still prone to fits of panic and at times irrational worry. I still struggle with "The Patty Pleaser" inside me, but I think many of us do. Whenever I walk by a bunch of laughing girls, I think they are laughing at me. The hair on the nape of my neck stands on end and I am transported back to the terror of the high school hallway sleeper cells. The sound of a siren sends me to dark places, I am the personification of a walking, open root-canal and I am terrified of dying when I turn forty-eight. The simple fact is, I have in the past twenty two years, cleaned myself up, wiped off the tarnish and even on occasions been downright shiny like new, but the distorted image I saw all those years ago in my mother's kitchen knife is etched like a scar and I have never been fully repaired.

I cannot say that I would even want to be repaired. I am what I am now. I would not have done anything different. I cannot say that it was all horror, because it wasn't. I cannot say that the experience was devoid of beauty, because beauty did exist. It existed in the moments, the tiny moments when one sees another's spirit, another's true essence. There were moments of great, open-mouthed laughter and genuine fun. There were moments of tenderness so gentle that our heartbeats slowed and our breath was held and our bodies felt light and in those brief moments, I swear we felt the presence of God.

It's in that presence, in that very silence that I learned something all those years ago. I know something. I think I know what life is. What it *really* is. What it *really* is about: although in the minutia of every day living that knowledge may fall by the wayside, may be hidden deep beneath life's quotidian trash, I now realize that it is as much a part of me as my bones and skin. I would not, could not trade what I know.

I see my father daily. When I look at my daughters I know he sent them to me, because when I look at them, oh God, how I feel him. How I understand his love for Matthew and me and how I hear the clickclickclick of his heart taking pictures of us as fast as the heart can feel, quick, quick before the eye blinks. So I too am taking pictures, clickclickclick, because it is all too fleeting, all too spotty, like my dream from long ago and I need to remember before the film spools out.

I want to remember each moment, each smile, each tantrum, each first, each "huggle," each "smooch," each giggle, each "I love you, Mommy."

Because, that's what I learned…

It all happens in the heartbeat.

It all happens in the blink.

Hey, Dad, I am paying attention.

"I have watched you take shape from a jumble of parts
And find the grace and form of a fine piece of art
Hey, You, my brand new woman, newly come into her
own
Don't you know that you don't need to grow up all alone."

"Tangled Up Puppet"
Harry Chapin

Endnotes

[1] Sarton , May. "Personal Letter." 25 September 1989. Print.

[2] Chopin, Kate. *I Wanted God. The Complete works of Kate Chopin*. Edited by Per Seyersted. Lousiana State University Press, 1969.

[3] Anonymous or courtesy of my NY Writer/Director. He inscribed it in a Shakespeare Anthology for me in 1994.

[4] Parker, Dorthy. *Symptom Recital. Enough Rope*. New York: Boni and Liveright, 1927.

[5] Herbert, Victor, Composer. "Toyland." Lyrics. Glen MacDonough. 1903. Song from: Operetta *Babes in Toyland*.

[6] Dorfman, Sid, writer. "The Army Navy Game." *MASH*. 20th Century Fox / CBS: 25 Feb 1973. Television.

[7] Mankiewicz, Joesph L., writer. "All About Eve." Warner Brothers: 1950. Film.

[8] Houseman, A. E. (1896). *To An Athlete Dying Young. A Shropshire Lad* . Kegan Paul, Trench, Trübner, & Co.

[9] Fitzgerald , F. S. (1920). *This Side of Paradise.* Scribner.

Acknowledgments

First off, let's get one thing straight… To everyone I have mentioned in this book, named or otherwise alluded to, to my family and my friends and to everyone I have ever crossed paths with during the last 33 years…I love you all. It took a village to grow me up and each one of you -- and you know who you are -- had a very strong hand in raising me. You are all the colors of my Carole King'esque "Tapestry." I am of you all and I am proud and honored to have known you or made out with you.

To my past…

To Dr. Howard Reiser, the late Dr. Joseph Ransohoff, Dr. Nancy Epstein and all the doctors who took care of my father, thank you. Because of all of you, I learned the difference between doctors who treat disease and true healers who treat the entire human being. I have chosen my own doctors accordingly and because of you.

Dr. Lori Ransohoff… Thank you for your blessing.

Aunt Lynn and Uncle Jon…Where would Matthew and I be without your guidance, the odd $100.00 bill that found its way into our pockets and the endless phone calls of support? I love you both.

Gils… You have no idea what you did for me the day you befriended me. Not only did you tell me the cardboard is not part of the tampon, which was a good piece of advice, but you loved me and took me with you in this journey of life.

Kent… I bitched and moaned, but you gave me stability. I learned a lot within your ivied tentacles and you let me be "me." I adored all my teachers and feel privileged to be the beneficiary of their knowledge. If you weren't so fucking expensive and my husband would let our daughters go to boarding school, I would happily and proudly send them your way.

Aiden, Kevin and George…You were good to me. You cared. You gave me so much. Thank you. If my heart were a timeshare, you'd all be living there together.

My Actor…I am glad you were my bridge to finding my happy.

My NY Writer/Director…You meant a lot to me. You gave when I couldn't. Thank you.

Professor John Bell at NYU, you were the first person to tell me I was smart. I hope I've proved you right. Thank you.

Colin Quinn…Thanks for making my father laugh.

To my *Remote Control* and *Another World* families and Natalie Hart, thank you.

Abby Sheeline… The very first reader, the very first believer. Thank you.

Margaret Staib… You have always been my friend. Your postivity is inspiring. Thank you for your support.

To my present…

Dr.'s Berkman, Katz, Share, Sparago, Ban and Weinberg…I have A LOT of shit and you all deal with it, sort it and heal it. Bless you.

To Jennifer L. Solari and Lisette Azar at CBS Publicity…Thank you for the *Jericho* photos and for your support. I am grateful.

Valerie Mayhew… You are my literary Guru. Thank you for your friendship, for your editing, the endless phone calls and for your knowledge of punctuation and story telling.

Stephanie Sloane… Thank you for your editing skills and your words of great encouragement. I am grateful.

Jessica Lauren… Who knew getting threaded at Fantastic Sam's would get my book published and I would make a new friend, which is no small feat in this world. Thank you.

Kathy Eldon and Amy Eldon Turteltaub… Thank you for your support and friendship. It means everything to me.

Ned… *The Good Red Road* took me many places. I thank you for holding me up, for knowing me now, for loving my husband and loving my girls. We love you.

Skeet Ulrich and Brad Beyer… Thank you for letting me use your gorgeous faces in *Gracefully Gone*. I adore you both.

Tim Omundson and George Newburn… you guys get me. Your support means the world.

Libby Allen… Thanks for reminding me of my younger self's voice.

Jeff Witjas… You have always supported me, always believed. Thank you.

Leslie Allan Rice… My Sister, my Friend, and my Manager. You believe even when I don't. You are to me like Gatsby's green light, my own constant source of hopeful illumination. Thank you for keeping me in the light.

Linda Dano, Christine Tucci, Michelle Hurd, The Holy Trinity of friends who truly are of Another World -- Grandmother and Godmothers to my daughters. Thank you for all the support, personal and professional. It is a scary thought to wonder where I'd be without you.

Sandy Chapin and The Chapin Family… It is all a circle, isn't it? Thank you for trusting me with Harry's words.

Matthew… We did it and then some. God bless us. I adore you.

Mom… It's not personal. It is what it is and only what it is. As Olivier would say… "Linda! Live the Life!" I love you.

Anthony… You are all. All that was. All that ever will be. Like taming a feral cat, you made a wife and mother out of me. I love you more than you know.

Mila, Esmé and Greta… You slay me. You own me. My father, your grandfather, yes Esmé, the one who is dead, would swoon over you. You are perfection. You are the reason I exist. There is no other. My love for you is crazy.

Daddy… As if the past 20 years of working on this doesn't ensure my love for you…Soap Operas are cool. So are potato chips, dill pickles in tuna sandwiches, ice cream sundaes from Friendly's and journals fused together to tell our story. I hope you are proud. You hung the moon.

To me… I am exhausted and I have a stomachache.

About the Authors

I am a mother to three little girls, Mila, Esmé and Greta. This is my hardest job and the one for which I am most grateful. My daughters are my heart and my (insert wink here) "career." My vacation so to speak is when I get to go to work as an actress.

You know me from CBS's *Jericho,* the only television show in a decade to be renewed after cancellation due to popular fan response. You also know me from the 141 episodes of primetime television that I have done in my twenty-year career: From the role of Lorna Devon on NBC's long running soap opera *Another World* for which I was nominated twice and won the Soap Opera Digest Award for Outstanding Younger Leading Actress to starring in television series such as TNT's *Bull,* NBC's *Cold Feet,* to name a few. I am highly recognizable for my roles in CBS's *CSI* and *Two And A Half Men,* NBC's *Law And Order; Criminal Intent, Crossing Jordan,* USA's *SUITS* and the feature film *National Treasure 2, Book Of Secrets.* I have recently recurred on ABC FAMILY's *Nine Lives Of Chloe King* and USA's *Common Law.* You will see me very soon playing Talia Hale in the much anticipated flashback episode of MTV's *Teen Wolf* about which I am very excited. It brings me back to my home network where I began my career during my college years at NYU, as the hostess of the iconic popular MTV game show *Remote Control* alongside co-host Colin Quinn.

You also might know my voice as I have an extensive voice over career, as the tag voice of *Acura,* the voice of *Kikkoman,* the trailer of Pedro Almodovar's *Volver,* and "She

Hulk" in the *Iron Man* games to name just a few.

There is more writing to come from me, much of which is influenced by my other career as wife and mother to my three daughters.

I am from Long Island, NY and hold a Bachelors Degree from NYU in Political Anthropology and Philosophy. You can imagine as an actress, mother, cook, laundress, Soccer Sherpa, and writer how very much that degree is used. I live in California with my wonderful husband and our three daughters.

My father was Matthew Louis Coppola Sr. He was born October 30, 1942 and died January 13, 1991. Everything in between these dates was a life well lived and well loved. According to the people who knew him best my father had a great sense of humor and a childlike sense of fun. He was a great athlete, a hard worker and a terrific friend. He was a pied piper to all children, a supportive, loyal husband, a dreamer, an actor and a present, fair and loving parent.

He made his living working for my grandfather in our family owned welding company, General Welding and later after his surgery he opened his own commercial photography studio, Coppola Creative Corp. I am not sure of the details of his jobs, as I was a child and don't remember much, but something tells me that although he made money doing those jobs, they were not his passion. I think being diagnosed with brain cancer at the all too early age of thirty-eight reprioritizes one's passion and perhaps he found that in us, my mom, my brother and me.

What I know about my father for sure is how he made me feel: safe, supported, cared for and loved. Anyone who ever knew him during his life felt the same. We were all fortunate and better for knowing him.

Made in the USA
San Bernardino, CA
23 May 2017